About the Author

PAMELA REDMOND SATRAN is the author of five novels and the co-author of many bestselling baby-name books (including the classic *Beyond Jennifer & Jason, Madison & Montana* and the brand-new *Beyond Ava & Aiden*). She writes for the *New York Times*, the Huffington Post and the Daily Beast; co-authors a monthly column for *Glamour*; and is a developer of nameberry.com. The founder of the 800-member group Montclair Editors and Writers, she lives in New Jersey with her husband and family.

HOW NOT TO ACT OLD

ALSO BY PAMELA REDMOND SATRAN

Fiction

The Home for Wayward Supermodels

Suburbanistas

Younger

Babes in Captivity

The Man I Should Have Married

Nonfiction

1,000 Ways to Be a Slightly Better Woman

Beyond Ava & Aiden

Cool Names for Babies

Beyond Jennifer & Jason, Madison & Montana

The Baby Name Bible

HOW NOT
TO ACT
OLD

185 Ways to Pass for Cool, Sound,
Wicked, or at Least Not
Totally Lame

PAMELA REDMOND SATRAN

Collins

Published in 2010 by Collins

HarperCollins Publishers
77–85 Fulham Palace Road,
London, W6 8JB

www.harpercollins.co.uk

First published in the USA by HarperCollins,
10 East 53rd Street, New York in 2009

10 12 14 13 11
1 3 5 7 9 10 8 6 4 2

Text © Pamela Redmond Satran 2009

Pamela Redmond Satran asserts her moral right to
be identified as the author of this work.

A catalogue record for this book
is available from the British Library.

ISBN 978-0-00-730613-8

Printed and bound in Great Britain by
Clays Ltd, St Ives plc

Mixed Sources

For my father
Joe Redmond
for ever ageless

Contents

Introduction

OK, so you go to the gym, but do you Tweet? You don't wear orthopaedic shoes, but can you grind? You own a mobile phone, but do you make calls with your index finger and leave voice mails?

If so, you may be acting older – a lot older – than you think you are.

I know, I know, you believed it would never happen to you. You thought you'd be cool for ever. And then, seemingly overnight, the evil young changed all the rules and you're left feeling . . . well, definitely something other than awesome.

Don't worry. The point here isn't to act like a twenty-six-year-old: God forbid. It's just to learn how not to act like somebody a twenty-six-year-old might snicker at. Or, failing that, at least to know *when* you're doing or saying something that might be construed as a mite over the hill – even if you don't want to change it.

Fans of hownottoactold.com will find this book features two-thirds all-new material, information that's never appeared on the website. And fans of the book should check in regularly at the site to find up-to-the-minute bulletins on how to keep not acting ancient.

We may be older than them. And tireder, saggier, crankier and more overwhelmed. We might be loath to wax our nether regions or adopt the thong – but at least when we act old, we'll know we're doing it.

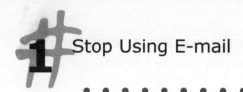

Stop Using E-mail

Leave it to the evil young to get all of us old people addicted to e-mail, and then to abandon the form in favour of texting and Facebook. Like bikini waxing (more on that later), e-mail is proving to be one of the Great Age Divides. Old people can't figure out why anyone would text, IM, or Facebook (wait: is that a verb?) instead of e-mail; how can you be articulate while typing with your thumbs? Why would you want everything you say to be public?

And young people hate e-mailing because it's . . . old.

Well, I don't care if e-mail is old; I can't stop using it. That's right, I'm addicted to e-mail, just as I am to dark chocolate after lunch and nitrous oxide at the dentist. I joined LinkedIn and Facebook and all those other services, and now I don't know what to do with them – or on them – or however you say it. So if you want to get in touch with me, send me an e-mail.

Just make sure it doesn't look like this one:

HOW NOT TO E-MAIL OLD: 10 MUSTS TO AVOID

12 July, 2009[1]
Dear Pam,[2]

Thank you for inviting me to your party.[3]

Unfortunately,[4] I will not be able to attend as I'll be having my false teeth fitted that day. My teeth had been bothering me for quite some time.

You know how it is when your gums start receding and then you crack a tooth or two chomping away on sweets. Next thing you know you need a root canal, and then a crown, and then it's just a house of cards in there.[5]

That's what happened to me, and so I found this dentist, Dr Marino, who said he'd pull them all out for just £4,000, which sounded like a bargain to me, so I told him . . .[6]

So write back and tell me what's going on with you.[7]

Your friend,[8]
Don[9]

www.donjenson.com[10]

---

1. Redundant, since all e-mails are date-stamped.
2. E-mails don't need a formal salutation, *à la* the letters you learned to write in primary school.
3. Nice, but capitalization, full sentences and formal statements like this just say old, old, old.
4. Proper punctuation? Actual paragraphs? We don't think so.
5. Too much information! Don't you know e-mails are public documents?
6. Zzzzzzz. This got way too long two paragraphs ago.
7. Sure, and I'll send it via carrier pigeon.
8. Not anymore.
9. We know.
10. Very gauche to include your own website. Better: barackobama.com or boston.com/bigpicture/, aka a site you love or a cause you believe in.

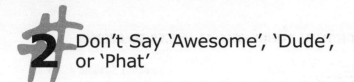

2 Don't Say 'Awesome', 'Dude', or 'Phat'

Slang is basically a shorthand way to let other people know how old you are. The problem is it doesn't work as simply and directly as you might think.

Using too-young slang, for instance, can very easily backfire and make you seem older, not younger, than you are. It's akin to wearing a yellow miniskirt or driving a Zipcar; you're trying too hard to be comfortable with something that was obviously minted by and for a generation that came way after yours.

The word awesome is a prime example. Few people over the age of forty can say 'awesome' in what sounds like their native tongue. For the most part, if you're older than forty, don't even attempt to say anything more modern than 'cool'.

Of course, you also don't want to swing too far the other way and use outmoded words like keen, neat, or smart.

It goes without saying that you must avoid such adolescent and hipster lingo as *phat*, *fierce* and *dope*. Even typing those words makes me feel a little sick, and I mean that in the old-fashioned, barfy sense of the word.

It may, however, be possible to successfully straddle the young–old slang divide and come up with something both cool and age-free by using outmoded words with confidence and irony. Groovy!

GUIDE TO 11 YOUNG–OLD SLANG EXPRESSIONS

YOUNG	OLD	SO OLD IT'S YOUNG AGAIN
Dude	Man	Baby
Sick	Cool	Groovy
Ugly bad	Coyote ugly	Sick
Feel	Dig	Grok
Bitch	Babe	Bird
Hot	Sexy	Dish
Fly	Cute	Suave
Ho	Old Lady	Wifey
Weed	Pot	Reefer
Durge	Creep	Fink
Whip me	Can I hitch a ride?	Can I get a lift?

3 Unstrap that Rolex

• • • • • • • • • • • • • • • • • •

'What?' you ask. 'What's the problem with my watch? Ohhhh, maybe it's that I'm not supposed to wear something so *expensive* strapped around my wrist. I guess that's the thing that makes me look old, bourgeois and overly self-satisfied.'

Well, yeah, except that's not really the problem. The problem is wearing any watch at all. The young do not wear watches. In fact, a naked wrist has become as emblematic of youth as ungrey hair and a perky butt.

Young people use their mobile phones to tell the time, and if you want to seem young, you should too. Just remember to flip your phone open or light it up with one hand, and to use your thumb – not your index finger – to do whatever it is you need to do. And try to make out the numbers without having to put on your glasses.

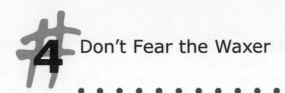

Don't Fear the Waxer

Listen, you can have all the work in the world done. You can get Botoxed and Restalyned till you're smooth as a balloon; you can have your boobs lifted to your chin and your tummy tucked into your backbone.

But if you don't wax down there, anybody who gets close enough – and that includes the entire changing room at the gym – is going to know you're old.

Waxing is one of the major differences between young and older women. We came of age feeling it was sacrilegious to so much as pluck one hair; they decided to shear most of it off. And even when we thought maybe we'd surprise our husbands for our twentieth anniversary, we were nervous. We saw *The 40-Year-Old Virgin*, after all. We knew it was going to hurt, plus be embarrassing, plus who knew what kind of diseases we might pick up.

If you're a Waxing Virgin, don't be afraid. It's not that bad. And the alternative is even worse: old below the belt.

40-YEAR-OLD BIKINI-WAXING VIRGIN? 9 THINGS TO EXPECT

1. **The waxer** will be waaaay more comfortable than you. After all, she's done this lots of time before.
2. **While it's not strictly necessary** to trim your pubic hair before you get waxed, waxing is easier if the hair is shorter to begin with, so you may want to get a head start.
3. If you're getting an **American wax** – which is just a basic clean-up – you can leave your panties on. The waxer may

twist and/or knot them to leave the sides of your groin area exposed for waxing.

4. **A French wax** is, technically, when you take most of the hair off, leaving only a 'landing strip' down the centre front, which can be anywhere from a thin line to a couple of inches wide.

5. **A Brazilian**, which you've undoubtedly heard about, is technically getting it all taken off – though you can also specify a Brazilian with a landing strip, which some people call a (yuck) Mohawk.

6. **The varying terminology** means you can't just resort to some euphemistic shorthand such as 'I'd like a Brazilian' and be sure you're not going to walk out of there looking like a plucked chicken. Unfortunately, at least the first time, you're going to have to spell it all out.

7. **Does it hurt?** Yes, though a couple of aspirin taken a half hour before can help. Lotion or baby powder and wearing a soft pair of tracksuit bottoms instead of stiff jeans home from the salon is also advised.

8. **The big question:** Why do it? Sex, baby. Assuming you're not parading around regularly in a string bikini, feeling sexier – and looking hotter – is the only conceivable rationale for a bikini wax.

9. **The bigger downside:** if you like it, you're going to have to keep doing it. How often? As frequently as every three or four weeks. Ouch!

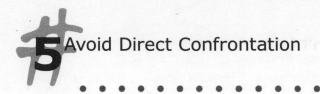

5 Avoid Direct Confrontation

• •

Maybe it's this silent, desktop world we inhabit. Maybe it's the new culture of positivity and triumph over depression. But having a big confrontation, complete with shouting, threats, revelations and tears, is a decidedly old, out-of-it thing to do.

If young people want to drop you or stop seeing you, they'll just stop returning your messages. Or defriend you on Facebook. If they're angry about something you've done to them, they'll blog about it. Or send topless pictures of you on their mobile phones to all their friends. I'm not kidding.

So what do you do if you have a problem with someone young? First, do some deep breathing, take a yoga class, smoke a joint, drink a martini – whatever you need to do to get in a more, ahem, relaxed mood. Then, if you must raise the issue, do so electronically, couched in passive-aggressive – or even passive-passive – language. Say you're having some 'issues' with the 'process'. Or rather, say 'I'm wondering whether you're having an issue with our process?'

Question marks at the end of every sentence are good. Then, if the other person responds, don't reply. Or take at least twice as long to respond as he or she took in the first place. If you're as wise as you should be by your age, you'll learn to keep your mouth shut until the problem disappears by itself . . . or the offending young person moves away.

6 Don't Leave a Message

This is a weird one, contributed by my nineteen-year-old son Joe. Only old people leave voice mails, says Joe. Young people, accustomed to communicating by mobile phone rather than landline, figure that their missed connections will see their number in missed calls and return the call if they want or need to talk. Urgent message? Send a text.

Since discovering this tip, I and several other old people of my acquaintance have tried it with amazing results. Before, when I had something important to tell a student or an assistant or a child, I'd leave a long, detailed voice message on her mobile phone . . . and never get called back.

Then I tried leaving a short, detailed message: 'Call me as soon as you get this.'

Maybe three days later, I'd hear from her – when I'd forgotten why I called in the first place.

Then I started using the magic technique. Say nothing. Just hang up. And like magic, the young people in my life started returning my calls instantly.

What this tells us:

- Unlike you, when a young person doesn't answer his mobile phone, it's not because he a) didn't hear it, b) forgot to charge it, or c) left it in his other bag. When a young person doesn't answer his mobile phone, it's because he saw your name and number on the screen and didn't want to talk to you.

- If you leave a detailed message, she'll be so annoyed that she won't listen to the message, nor will she call you back because she'll be under the illusion that she's already talked to you – or, more precisely, that you've already talked to her.

- If you say nothing, you'll be speaking his language (see #77: Don't Fear the Silence). Plus, he'll get nervous that what you have to tell him is so bad or so good you couldn't leave it on voice mail. Plus, he'll be curious. And he'll call you back.

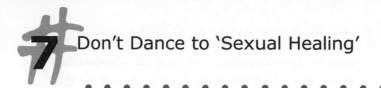

Don't Dance to 'Sexual Healing'

Dancing to a sexy song – especially an *old* sexy song – is probably all right as long as there aren't any other people around – particularly any young people. But if young people are watching, attempting to get lost enough in moving to the music to enjoy it, much less be any good at it, will be impossible. All that snickering will make you too self-conscious.

Plus, you know, sexy dancing is different these days. Instead of face-to-face, people dance doggy-style. The unsubtle-yet-accurate name for this kind of dancing is 'grinding'. I really don't think this is something you want to attempt in public – at least, *I* don't want to see it – but in the privacy of your own home, you might want to give it a go.

HOW TO GRIND, IN 6 EASY STEPS

1. If you are a woman, stand by yourself and move your hips in a figure eight motion. Look bored and unfocused, not smiling or making eye contact with anyone – as if you were, say, wiping down the kitchen counters.

2. If you are a man, approach the casually dancing woman from behind. Touching her hips, press your pelvis lightly against her buttocks and begin moving in rhythm with her, following her lead. Do not make any untoward thrusting motions, and try not to act as if this is the most exciting thing that has happened to you since you were fourteen.

3. Continue rotating your hips in tandem. The woman in front can raise her arms or hold them out to the side while dancing. The gentleman behind her can touch her hips and stomach or run his hands up and down her sides, though all this touching must be done gently, never forcefully. Basically, touch as if you'd just met the person, not as if your penis had taken up residence in her butt.

4. Partners can switch positions, with the woman grinding against the man's behind. Front-to-front grinding is, however, usually discouraged.

5. Men, if you get an erection – and really, if you don't, you're so old you're beyond the help of this book – move subtly away or at least adjust yourself so that it's not poking into her. Remember, you are so cool that even publicly rubbing your genitals against a stranger's hindquarters leaves you completely unfazed.

6. If one partner wants to stop grinding, just walk away. The remaining partner can and should keep dancing as if nothing has happened.

8 BEST OLD-PEOPLE SONGS TO DANCE TO . . .

If, like me, you can't stop dancing to old sexy songs, at least pick the right old sexy songs. Here, some great ones:

1. 'Let's Get It On', Marvin Gaye
2. 'Boogie Nights', Heatwave
3. 'Love Train', The O'Jays
4. '(Love Is Like a) Heat Wave', Martha and the Vandellas
5. 'Sex Machine', James Brown
6. 'Billie Jean', Michael Jackson
7. 'RESPECT', Aretha Franklin
8. 'Night Fever', The Bee Gees

AND 7 YOUNG ONES THAT MAY ACTUALLY GET YOU GOING

1. 'Don't Stop the Music', Rihanna
2. 'Shake That Thing', Sean Paul
3. 'Toxic', Britney Spears
4. 'Crazy in Love', Beyonce
5. 'D.A.N.C.E.', Justice
6. 'Yeah!', Usher
7. 'Hot in Herre', Nelly

8–19 How Not to Work Old

Want to get and keep your job without being labelled old, aka tired and out-of-it? Here's how not to act old at work:

#8 Don't Arrive at the Crack of Dawn and make everybody feel guilty for not being there as early as you. If you're bushy-tailed and at your desk by 6:35, at least have the good grace to keep your mouth shut about it.

#9 Don't Bring the Doughnuts. You don't need to be Mummy or Daddy to the entire office, showing up with coffee, remembering all the birthdays, making sure everybody signs the card.

#10 Don't Punch the Clock. Of course, you may have to punch an actual clock at your workplace, but we mean this more metaphorically. Don't treat your job like a prison where you're just putting in your time.

#11 Stifle the Self-aggrandizing Anecdotes. Reminiscing about the year you almost won the Pulitzer or that time you saved the company a million pounds won't convince people you're cooler than they already think you are.

#12 Don't Be Tough. The young approach is much softer and less direct. People ask questions and seem to defer to others even when they have a strong opinion. And if they want to do it their way anyway, they'll just go ahead without discussion or confrontation.

#13 **Keep It Zipped** – and I don't mean just your mouth. Don't think that just because you got the memo about sexual harassment that your behaviour is squeaky clean. Making off-colour jokes, talking about your personal life, asking your co-workers about last night's date, or commenting on someone's clothes or body is not only inappropriate but kind of gross. And girlfriends, don't think you're exempt here.

#14 **No Sexist or Racist Jokes.** And that includes mild, veiled, or oh-so-ironic ones.

#15 **Don't Stay Glued to Your Chair.** Rolling everywhere, avoiding getting up and walking across the room and sitting there till your arse grows around the cushion is definitely acting old – and won't do much for the way you look, either.

#16 **No Long-range Planning.** Looking too far ahead, wanting firm commitments on times and places far (i.e. more than a day or two) into the future, is definitely an old thing. If you simply must plan (I know I must), do it in secret and be flexible if things change.

#17 **Don't Be a Human Archive.** There may be value in having someone at a company who can detail the CVs of everyone who has held a job there since 1981, who can remember what year manual typewriters were upgraded to electrics and when secretaries were replaced by voice mail. But there isn't much value in letting that person be you.

#18 **No Packed-lunching It.** Carrying your lunch to work in tupperware suggests that you a) have actual food in your house and b) care more about pinching a few pennies than you do about going out with your co-workers or eating something interesting – or even skipping lunch to maintain your boyish figure. Packed lunches are for people old enough to have mortgages and kids' tuitions to worry about . . . which is why this is probably one HNTAO rule you'll delight in breaking.

#19 **It's Not All about the Job.** Young people may work more hours and seem more tireless, but they're also into kayaking, hanging out with their dogs, playing *bocce* at the hipster bar and meeting other attractive young people. Getting too excited about your work – or seeming excited about work to the exclusion of everything else – will make you seem old.

20 Beware the Accidental Hook-up

Admit it: you don't really know what 'hook-up' (or 'hookup' or 'hook up') means. Is it meeting for coffee? Kissing? Having sex? Watching television together? Getting engaged?

The point is that you should avoid using the term if you're not certain of its implications. As cool and casual as it may make you feel, it's probably best not to suggest to your boss that you hook up later on this evening. Maybe not smart to ask your teenager whether he hooked up with any of his friends last night. Might not be wise to say wistfully to your neighbour that you wish you could hook up more often.

So what *does* hook-up mean? Anything and everything, apparently. Maybe if we get under the covers and turn out the lights for long enough, the phrase and all its implications will just go away.

WHAT EXACTLY IS A HOOK-UP? A TEENAGER TELLS ALL . . . WELL, SOME

What is this 'hook-up' we've been hearing so much about? When you say that two people are 'hooking up', what does that mean, exactly? To find out, we asked our resident teenager.

Old Person: What does hook-up mean?
Teenager: I don't know. It could mean anything.
OP: Going to the movies? Meeting for coffee?
Teen (smirking): Not that.
OP: What then? Having sex?
Teen: Gross! Stop!

OP: So hooking up is not necessarily having sex?

Teen: No.

OP: So if I said to Dad, 'Let's hook up later –'

Teen: No! You can't say that!

OP: Okaaaaaaaaaaay. So it might not always mean sex, but it always means something like sex.

Teen: Not necessarily.

OP: So can it mean dating?

Teen: Dating?

OP: I mean hanging out. Going out with someone.

Teen: Maybe.

OP: So have you ever hooked up with anyone?

Teen: Leave me alone!

21 Don't Smoke Pot

It's not the smoking of marijuana that's the problem, exactly. In fact, if you know where to get some, can you please let me know? No, the problem is calling it 'pot'. Pot is what old hippies called it. What we called it when we used to smoke it every day. Nowadays, it's called 'weed'. I think.

22 Don't Fear the F-word

I vividly remember the first time I encountered the f-word. I was six, newly proficient on a two-wheeler and taking an independent spin around the block when there it was, chalked right on the asphalt. I had never heard or seen this word before, but it must mean something important, I thought, to be written there in such big letters.

So I rode home and asked my father, who was sitting on our front steps, what 'fuck' meant. And the next thing I knew, my father walloped me across the face.

Dad didn't hit; that's part of the reason his slap still stings nearly half a century later. In fact, Dad rarely even got angry. And my parents, New Yorkers who'd grown up in rough neighbourhoods, freely used 'bad words' – shit, damn, bitch and bastard – all the time.

But fuck was different, even apart from that slap in the face. It wasn't spoken, it wasn't written and you didn't hear it on TV or in the lyrics of songs. It wasn't used as a curse, not even by adults who had been drinking when they didn't think the kids were listening, and it wasn't used to describe the sexual act either.

In fact, the f-word was for decades literally outlawed in both the United States and Britain, and was omitted from standard dictionaries and encyclopedias. A typically wonderful history of the word can be found in The Online Etymological Dictionary, and Wikipedia and YouTube also include educational information on the use and misuse of the f-word over time.

But when did everyone from the mum next door to the guy you're negotiating a business deal with start saying 'fucking' and

'I'm fucked' and 'fucked-up' as routinely as people once said 'darn' or 'screw'? When did teenage kids and their parents start saying it to each other without so much as a blink, never mind a slap? Maybe around the time Tony Soprano appeared on HBO, or *Four Weddings and a Funeral* hit the cinemas, or the Notorious B.I.G. started singing on the radio. Yes, I'm blaming the media – not for creating the trend, but for letting us all know it was okay to use that particular word now and again. And again.

Does that mean that, in the interest of not acting old, you should use the f-word more liberally? I find it pretty fucking expressive, myself . . . though I can never say it without flinching just a little bit.

#23–29 How Not to Weekend Old

• • • • • • • • • • • • • • • • •

#23 Don't Go Home after Work on Friday. Instead, head to the nearest bar with colleagues and knock back enough drinks to achieve oblivion.

#24 Don't Maintain Professional Distance between Yourself and that Hot Colleague. Once oblivion has been achieved, you can retreat to a dark corner and 'accidentally' start making out. You didn't plan it! Nothing really happened! On Monday you'll both act as though it were but a dimly remembered dream.

#25 Don't Bounce out of Bed on Saturday Morning. Sleep late. Keep sleeping. Zzzzzzz. If it's before noon, you must stay horizontal.

#26 No Chores. Forget any notion that weekends are for catching up on laundry, going food shopping, cleaning the bathroom, cooking for the week ahead, paying bills, or anything else 'productive'. Weekends are for playing video games, shooting hoops, doing sun salutations, shopping for shoes, or sleeping on the beach.

#27 Don't Stay Home on Saturday Night. You don't want to be home in your tracksuit bottoms with your feet up, drinking a nice glass of Scotch and watching the first season of *Mad Men*, do you? Shut up, you do not! No, you want to be wearing a sequined miniskirt and high-heeled sandals and going to a club!

You want to be playing pool, knocking back vodka jelly shots and dancing to My Chemical Romance!

#28 Do Not Read the Sunday Paper. As a journalist, this one physically pains me. But the fact is that while almost everybody over forty reads the Sunday paper as religiously as our parents went to church, most younger people don't bother, believing that if anything truly important happens, the universe will text them the news.

#29 Don't Cook Dinner for the Family. Invite the grandparents, the aunt and uncle, and their kids over for Sunday dinner? Roast a chicken, bake some brownies, spend all day first getting the house ready for guests and then cleaning up after them? That's for people who believe in sacrificing themselves for worthless rituals. And you, well, you have better things to do – like eat the brownies.

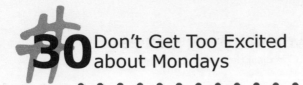

30 Don't Get Too Excited about Mondays

Hello, my name is Pam, and I am a Monday Lover. It's not that I don't like weekends, exactly. But at the weekends I spend a lot of time doing all those household chores – laundry, food shopping, weeding – I don't have time to do during the week. My husband and kids are around, wanting to be cooked for, driven around and sometimes even communed with.

And then on Monday morning, they all leave. I'm alone, free to work without distraction or interruption. I don't feel guilty about writing instead of going to the bookstore with my husband or making pasta for my son. And if I sometimes sneak out for lunch with a friend, it's nobody's business but my own.

But when I was young, weekends meant fun and freedom and sex, and Monday meant a return to drudgery and imprisonment in some stupid job. Would I go back to that time? No. I love loving Mondays. But I wouldn't mind loving Saturdays and Sundays a little bit more.

31 Avoid Avoiding Babies

• • • • • • • • • • • • • • • • • • • •

I know you're not a monster; it's just that you're sooooooo over the baby thing. You've already put in your time jollying the infant who started crying in the middle of the meal, bouncing the toddler up and down the aisle of the plane, being pinned beneath the child who refused to sit anywhere but your lap. And now you're ready for some freedom.

But avoiding babies is like admitting you hate kittens, or sunshine. Instead, you might try one of the following 10 great excuses.

I WOULD LOVE TO HOLD THE BABY, BUT . . .

- I'm having a herpes outbreak.
- I was just about to watch some porn.
- Perhaps I should first put on a rubber suit, since I'm coming from the infectious diseases quarantine unit.
- I'm so sorry, I'm allergic to babies.
- I've recently been handling a snake.
- I just ate some gorgonzola cheese. *Yes*, with my fingers.
- I'm very sad right now, and I don't think it would be good for the baby to see me sobbing.
- I have Tourette's Syndrome, and I wouldn't want my language to shock the baby.
- I have Restless Leg Syndrome, and I wouldn't want to bounce the baby right off my lap onto the floor.
- I'm pretty sure that baby wants to kill me.

32 Don't Be Proud of Being Befuddled by Technology

Sure, it's baffling. Of course, the mushrooming parade of applications like Digg, Reddit, Facebook, LinkedIn and Twitter is overwhelming. In fact, I sometimes suspect that half those things are not actually real but a plot by people under thirty-five to drive the rest of us insane.

But the important thing is not to admit how overwhelmed you are. 'I don't understand why anyone would use Facebook instead of e-mail' or 'We still don't know how to work the Sky+ box' are things you must not say out loud.

Above all, don't make a big public deal (ya know, like I am right now) of how clueless you are about using your computer as anything other than a glorified typewriter or working all those mysterious buttons on your TV.

Just quietly hire a fourteen-year-old boy as your tech consultant. Or act as if you're above the whole technology tsunami – you're so cool, you're unGoogleable! – rather than swamped by it. Use it, or don't use it. But don't act like it's cute to be befuddled by it.

WEB DIRECTORY 102: SITES YOU SHOULD KNOW

OK, we assume you've heard of the internet. You've Googled, you've probably even YouTubed. But what about the next layer of web use? Here are some sites that most young people know – and you should, too:

Boing Boing: boingboing.net is, according to technorati (more on that later), the world's most popular blog, full of tech tips, pop culture and curiosities.

Delicious (delicious.com): sometimes written as del.icio.us, a way to organize and share your bookmarks.

Digg (digg.com): a public place where you collect and rate your favorite websites and stories.

Etsy (etsy.com): a centre for buying and selling handmade goods.

Google Trends (google.com/trends): see the Top 100 searches right now.

Second Life (secondlife.com): a virtual world where your avatar does things you only dream about.

Technorati (technorati.com): lists which blogs and posts are getting how much attention when.

10 x 10 (tenbyten.org): an ever-changing array of one hundred words and pictures that define the moment.

Twitter (twitter.com): provides minute-by-minute mini-updates on what you and many others are doing, thinking, seeing, or planning.

Xanga (xanga.com): a social-networking site that lets the user create a personal profile, include music and graphics, and keep a public blog.

Yelp (yelp.com): a collection of user reviews of restaurants, shops and services.

#33 Don't Advise People to Carry an Umbrella

● ● ● ● ● ● ● ● ● ● ● ● ● ● ● ●

Stop telling otherwise-competent adults to pack an umbrella, wear a jumper, or go to the bathroom before they leave. You don't need to be the world's mum, always know better than everyone else, or take control of every task, no matter how mundane.

But what if, without your direction, your husband goes to work without his wallet and your daughter wanders out in the snow in her T-shirt and everyone within your orbit constantly has to go to the bathroom when there is no bathroom around?

Well, maybe such desperate circumstances will teach them to take a little more responsibility for themselves. If they turn around and try to blame their oversight on you, shame on them. And with all the energy you'll save once you stop nannying the entire world, you can do something really productive, like find a way to reverse the aging process.

16 THINGS YOU NEVER NEED TO SAY TO ANOTHER ADULT

1. Bring some money along if you're going out.
2. Are you sure you're going to be warm enough in that?
3. Don't drink too much.
4. Say thank you.
5. Don't stay out too late.
6. Lock the car.
7. Are you comfortable in those shoes?
8. You'd better wear a hat.

9. Is that coat warm enough?
10. Did you have enough to eat?
11. Did you brush your teeth?
12. Maybe you want to comb your hair.
13. If you don't hurry up, you're going to be late.
14. Do you have something to read while you're waiting?
15. Are you sure you have everything you need?
16. Are you sure?

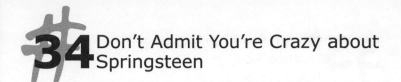

#34 Don't Admit You're Crazy about Springsteen

Dear Bruce: I'm so sorry. It kills me to say this. But I love you, and I know you'd want me to tell the truth as I see it deep in my heart. So as wonderful as you are, as much as I admire you, as much as I still love to dance and drive to your songs, I'm afraid that makes me seem old, at least in the eyes of the young.

It seems like just yesterday – though it was 1975 – that I first saw you onstage singing 'Born to Run'. You were so sexy; I went out with a guy in my writing class solely because he looked like you. Much more recently, I saw you shopping for earrings with Patty, who was much more gorgeous in real life than in pictures. I thought you still looked pretty hot – though a little less hot than you looked in 1975.

I don't know what's wrong with the Evil Young. You are obviously one of the musical geniuses of our age, constantly innovating and reinventing yourself, and I would have thought that if there were any aging rocker that the young could respect, it would be you.

But no. Say you love Bruce Springsteen, and the Evil Young give you the kind of look that says, 'Oh, you wear support hose rolled down below your knees? You boil your chicken because your teeth won't stand up to anything tougher? I think I'll just shove your shrivelled old carcass into this here ditch.'

The solution? Never, God forbid, stop listening to you, Bruce. Without you, how would we run, how we would dance, how, dear God, would we ever have sex? No, the solution is to just keep buying your music and listening to your songs in secret, hiding the evidence from our teenagers and junior colleagues, just like we did when we were thirteen and didn't want Mummy to know we were listening to Elvis.

35 Don't Be the Monica

• • • • • • • • • • • • • • • • • •

In many couples of whatever age, one person's the Chandler, and the other person is the Monica. One person is the Homer, and the other is the Marge. One person is Han Solo, and the other is Princess Leia. One person acts young, in other words: wacky, fun-loving, charmingly irresponsible. And the other person gets stuck with acting old.

(For those of you born after 1980, think Gaby and Carlos from *Desperate Housewives*. Or Paula Abdul and Simon Cowell.)

How do you become the Monica in your relationship? Well, someone's got to pay the bills. Organize the taxes. Discipline the children. Excuse me a sec: WOULD YOU PUT AWAY THAT ICE CREAM BEFORE WE GET ANTS ALL OVER THE COUNTER?

Where was I? Oh, right: the next thing you know, you're the Monica. You're yelling and screaming and cursing and threatening. You're managing the money and blowing your top when the credit card is maxed out, the mobile phone bill is through the roof and there are watermarks on the coffee table.

So tell me, who do you want to be: the screaming cheque-writer or the starry-eyed, golden-footed wookie-lover?

#36–44 How Not to Be a Cougar

OK, we get that you want to have sex with a twenty-seven-year-old. But that doesn't mean you need to tip over the edge into cougardom. How not to look and act like a predatory dame:

#36 No Animal Prints. Nothing says cougar like, well, a pair of leopard-print stilettos. Or a tiger-striped chiffon blouse, unbuttoned down to there.

#37 Bottle the Brassy Blonde. By all means, colour your hair. But even dye-it-at-home brews have progressed beyond brassy blonde and neon orange. Subtler is sexier.

#38 Watch the Cleavage. You may not notice this standing at home surveying yourself in the mirror, but when you lean over and press your arms together, that lovely cleavage turns into a gathering place for wrinkles.

#39 Dim the Bling. Tinkly earrings, swinging gold chains and clanking bracelets all cry out too loudly for attention.

#40 Lighten Up the Make-up. Heavy make-up often has the opposite effect from the one you intend – covering the wrinkles and the age spots, maybe, but making you look weirdly older in the process.

#41 Muffle the Guffaw. Middle-aged ladies out for a good time often laugh way too loudly, as if they haven't had this much fun in a long time and may never get the chance again. Note to self: must stop that.

#42 Watch the Sly Innuendo. As if your young prey haven't picked up on the fact that you were ready and available: slathering on the nudge-nudge, wink-wink references to anything physical or sexual is cougar overkill.

#43 Don't Dis the Babes. Making snide remarks about the all-around inferiority of younger women fools no one. All it says is that you're jealous and insecure. You are, too.

#44 Break Away from the Pack. Travelling with a mob of hungry girlfriends pretty much guarantees there won't be enough meat for anyone. (Hey! That's a sly innuendo!) Either act and look like you're really out for a night with the girls or do your hunting alone.

I think that's it, unless you still have any sense of fun and adventure left for me to kill.

45 Stop Talking about Menopause

There is a kind of girl who's always liked to talk about her period: how she can't wait to get it, when she's having it, how bad her cramps are, where she buys her tampons, whether she's late, how heavy her flow is, when it's slowing down and what it feels like when it stops altogether.

And to all that I say: *lalalalalalalalalalalalalalalalalalalala*. In other words, I don't want to hear about it, okay? When did menstruation, or the lack thereof, get to be a topic for polite conversation? I guess around the time they started running ads for tampons on prime-time TV. But to me it's just, ew, gross.

But it seems to me the only thing more boring and unseemly than discussing getting your period is discussing not getting your period. What's so interesting about menopause, anyway? What is this wisdom they keep talking about, this freedom, this huge change that demands hormones – or maybe not hormones – sorry, I can't keep track.

Some of you might say my position on this issue is old, and that the modern stance is to be openly affirmational about the feminine circle of life. Well, I can get all woman-y with the best of them, girlfriend, and I get that public is the new private. But I still say keep the whole blood-in-your-cooter thing to yourself.

46 No Lame Parenting Advice

· · · · · · · · · · · · · · · · · ·

We think, just because we've been through it all, that young parents want our advice about how to handle projectile vomiting, frozen-food-aisle temper tantrums, failing grades in history and curfew violations.

Well, they don't. They don't want our suggestions that they pick a normal name like William instead of a weird one like Wylie or Wyoming. They don't want to hear that day care doesn't work when your kid gets sick – and a kid in day care gets sick all the time. They don't want us to tell them to be firmer about saying no, or softer on television habits, or more involved with their careers and spouses and less with parenting.

They don't want to know what we think because it's all going to be different for them. They'll never get fat or grow bored staying home with the baby, they'll never fight with their spouse in front of the kids or lose their temper or realize way too late that they made a childrearing mistake. Their kids, unlike ours, will always want to go to school and do their homework, will never grow pimples or defriend them on Facebook. And if we do barge in and advise breastfeeding or public school or a generous allowance (or solid food, private school and no allowance), we turn ourselves into the meddling grandma, not only old but ignorant and interfering.

The solution? Zip it. Zip! Zip! It's not like keeping quiet will hurt you. And if everything really isn't different for them and they make lots of mistakes we might have saved them from, well, it just might be possible to get a certain pleasure from that, mightn't it?

19 THINGS NEVER TO SAY TO A YOUNG PARENT

1. Are you sure he's warm enough?
2. You named him *what??*
3. I think she's hungry.
4. Who do you leave him with when you go to work?
5. Maybe she should be wearing a hat.
6. Where is your husband?
7. Where is your wife?
8. Don't you worry that the dog might bite her?
9. Are those socks warm enough?
10. Is that stroller really comfortable?
11. I think . . . maybe . . . you need to change a nappy.
12. Wow, you look ready to pop!
13. When are you due? Whoops, I mean, you are pregnant, aren't you?
14. God, you look miserable.
15. God, I remember having little kids like that, and it was exhausting.
16. Are you ever going back to work?
17. So is this the last one?
18. How old are you now?
19. Once they're in school, then what?

47 Don't Fear the Tat

• • • • • • • • • • • • • • • • • • •

Tat is of course short for tattoo – and the truth is, I do fear them. The neck tattoo is to me what shaggy hair, elephant bells and leather jackets were to our parents: a sign of both danger and decay. Show me a neck tattoo, and I'll show you a pregnant fifteen-year-old who drinks Pepsi for breakfast and lives in a trailer with plumbing that drains into a wading pool.

Of course, I could show you a neck tattoo, and you might show me Victoria Beckham, aka Posh Spice, aka Mrs David Beckham. Or Eva Longoria, the Desperate Housewife who would never really live in the suburbs. Or Angelina Jolie, or Ben Affleck, or Amy Winehouse (there's a role model), or just about any contestant on any reality show – tattoos, neck or otherwise, seem to be a prerequisite for crossing the Hollywood town line.

Why would anyone get a tattoo? That's a very good question. In fact, let's do a Q & A on the subject with a noted authority, me:

Q: Why would anyone get a tattoo?
A: The young get tattoos for the sole purpose of setting themselves apart from the old. 'I'm nothing like you,' the tattoo signals, 'and I want to make sure the entire world knows it, so I'm going to etch this large blue and red symbol on my neck. Just so there's never any confusion. And I mean never, ever, ever.'

Q: Exactly! That's the problem with tattoos: they're so permanent! Why would anyone want to mark his body with a symbol of something or someone he might not care about in two decades – or even two months?

A: The young believe that who and what they are now, they will stay for ever, and the tattoo is evidence of a superstitious belief that making a permanent mark will create a permanent condition. Or at least that's what studies show. Or what I think.

Q: What's with the Asian ideogram thing? Why would a kid who's not Asian, has no desire to travel through Thailand or Mongolia, and can barely write and read English choose to put a Chinese character on her shoulder or forearm?
A: As with so much else, it's Angelina's fault. Right, Jen?

Q: Won't having a tattoo make it hard to get a good job? Look terrible if you want to wear a strapless wedding gown? Be difficult and painful to remove if you change your mind when you're thirty-five?
A: Yes! That's what I keep telling them! But nobody listens!

Q: But you're so intelligent! So right! Why won't they listen?
A: Because they think I'm old and out of it and that I don't know what I'm talking about and that they're never going to feel the way I feel or be the way I am. And my only consolation is knowing for sure what a fifty-year-old arse looks like, and why a fat red rose would not add anything to the picture.

8 TATTOOS FOR OLD PEOPLE

Old people can't get tattoos that say 'Mum' ('cause she's no longer around to appreciate it) or 'Winona For Ever' ('cause you broke up fourteen years ago) or 'Live Fast, Die Young' in Japanese ('cause you already didn't). Instead, you might consider these options:

- The Chinese symbol for 'overmortgaged'.
- Wedding ring with thorns sticking out of it.
- A rose, slightly wilted.
- Portrait of your teenage child with horns growing from his head.
- A cross to which you yourself have been nailed.
- An anchor, tied to your ankle.
- A heart with a mop stabbed through it.
- A solid patch of black on the arse: slimming!

48 Don't Make Love

It's not the act of copulation that's the problem; it's calling it 'making love'. Or 'sleeping with'. Or 'getting it on'.

When young people 'do it', they usually come right out and say 'having sex'. Or sometimes (see #20) 'hooking up'. Or sometimes, yes, 'fucking'.

'Bone', 'jump', and 'play' may be related words, but I know that only because I looked it up in the Online Slang Dictionary.

Whatever you call it, if you do it, you're not allowed to hate it. I'm talking to you, sisters, since I've never encountered a male of any age who hated sex. It's women over a certain age who complain about sex, avoid having sex and, deep down, just don't like it.

Naturally, this is a bigger problem than acting old. It's evidence of some heavy repression. Or maybe you hate your husband. Or perhaps you're orgasmically challenged. If you're seeing yourself in this paragraph, the solution may be to get yourself a vibrator and learn how to use it. (*Pssst*: babeland.com. Try the Acuvibe or Magic Wand.)

49 Do Not Block the Aisle

• • • • • • • • • • • • • • • • •

Blocking the aisle at the supermarket, standing smack in the middle of the pavement, spacing out on the buffet queue: why does this offense seem directly correlated with advancing age?

Every time I find myself stuck behind some wide-hipped matron in the canned soup aisle, I experience a frisson of age-related fury. God, I find myself thinking, that person is so old and out of it. While look at young, energetic me, agilely manoeuvring my trolley around bulky displays, deftly plucking items from the highest and lowest shelves, efficiently carrying out my errands.

Whoops, sorry. Excuse me. I guess I must have been spacing out there for a minute, wondering exactly why I came down this aisle in the first place. Now I remember, I was looking for pancake mix, but I couldn't find it. Oh, duh, the big red and yellow box, right there in front of me. I guess I was so absorbed in trying to find it that I didn't hear you coming up behind me.

And then instantly I'm the old, out-of-it person who can't see or hear or move or think well enough to even be aware that I'm blocking the aisle. The cure? Online food shopping.

50 Throw off the Middle-aged Burka

When exactly did the Imams sweep through my town in suburban New Jersey and decree that every woman over the age of forty had to chop off her hair, wash off her make-up and start dressing in baggy black or beige linen or flannel, buttoned up to the neck, hanging down to the ground – and I'll have you wear flat, rubber-soled shoes with that, missy?

The middle-aged, suburban, woman-shrouding style is so ubiquitous that anyone wearing something bright, tight, or low-cut (usually that's me) is viewed with suspicion. What's she up to? Who does she think she is? Where is she going? And why is she flaunting it like that?

I say break out the hair dye, invest in some really expensive undergarments and make your daughters take you shopping for once. If your husband feels threatened, if your friends think you're a traitor to the sisterhood, if the other mums question your fitness, let 'em. As long as you're still walking this earth, you might as well do it in shoes that click.

12 THINGS YOU CAN'T EVEN THINK ABOUT WEARING (FOR WOMEN)

1. Granny pants.
2. Granny glasses.
3. A slip.
4. Nude tights.
5. Smart shoes with rubber soles.

6. Tailored trousers with an elastic waist.
7. Blue eyeshadow.
8. Dangly earrings with long hair and glasses.
9. Mum jeans: if they come from BHS, cover your belly button and have a 'relaxed' fit, they're off-limits.
10. A turquoise or lilac cotton sweater.
11. A flowered chiffon scarf.
12. A fake leather handbag that's trying to pretend it's not fake.

As with everything, there are exceptions to these rules. But somehow, I'm guessing the items you own are not among them.

 No Poodles

There are 'young' dogs and there are 'old' dogs, and I'm sorry, but poodles are owned mainly by people over forty. Why? Because they're practical: smart, hypoallergenic, non-shedding. And because they're out of style.

The small dog *du jour* is a Yorkie or a Dachshund, not a toy poodle. The big dog favoured by hipsters might be a Labrador retriever, or even a Labradoodle, but never a standard poodle. The retro favourite breed could be a German shepherd, but won't be a poodle. In fact, poodles are so far out they may even be coming in. But owning one still won't do much for your Age Image.

PET MAKING YOU LOOK OLD? 5 SWAPS TO CONSIDER NOW

SWAP THIS OLD PET	FOR THIS YOUNG PET
Persian cat	Ocelot
Hamster	Rat
Donkey	Pony
Parakeet	Parrot
Goldfish	Piranha

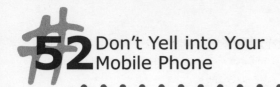

52 Don't Yell into Your Mobile Phone

• • • • • • • • • • • • • • • •

Old people talk into their mobile phones as if the phone was a tin can attached to a string, and the string was so long that the person with his ear pressed to the other tin can was in China.

Although mobile phones are extremely tiny and not connected to any wires, they're really more efficient than that. You can speak in a normal voice – no, in a softer-than-normal voice – and the other person will hear you. We promise.

Sssssh. That's better.

8 WAYS NOT TO PHONE OLD

1. Don't be unable to find your mobile phone because you put it away in a different place every time.

2. Don't hold your phone at arm's length – so you can read the numbers – and then dial very, very slowly, with your index finger.

3. Don't be afraid of your phone: learn to programme the speed dial, use the voice-activated and speed dialling, regulate the volume, even – wow! – use that tiny button on the side to flick off the ringer thing.

4. Don't be clueless about the other things besides making phone calls that your phone can do: texting, alarms and . . . gee, that's as far as I've got.

5. If you've figured out texting, adopt a few of the basic short-cuts: idk ('I don't know'), yt ('you there?'), cu ('see you'), ttyl ('talk to you later').

6. Don't hurry off the phone because you're afraid of running up your bill. You have eight hundred minutes a month, and you've used only sixty-three.

7. Do not set your ringtone to the *Sex and the City* theme or the old phone tone (*brrring brrring*).

8. Try not to suffer from mobile-phone deafness, aka the inability to hear your mobile phone ring or catch what the other person is saying unless you're in the equivalent of a soundproof booth.

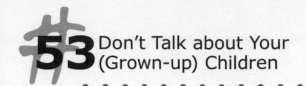# 53 Don't Talk about Your (Grown-up) Children

• • • • • • • • • • • • • • • • • •

Going to parties where all my contemporaries spent their time talking about their grown-up children instead of themselves, the world, or, God forbid, asking about me was what gave me the idea for this book. It's not the fact of *having* grown-up kids that makes you seem old. And of course you can mention what they're up to if asked. But going on and on about what your grown-up kids are doing, where they're living, and who they're dating makes it seem as if they're the ones who are doing all the interesting things now, while you – you're past your prime.

Unless you're, say, ninety-seven or Jon Voight – make that ninety-seven *and* Jon Voight – you don't want to stand in the shadow of your child's life *or* use her glory to enhance your own.

Maybe you need to do some more interesting things. Or think of something interesting to say about the regular old things you're doing. Or simply recognize that, even if you're not that fascinating, I'd still rather hear about you than your twenty-three-year-old, whom I haven't even seen since she was eleven and frankly never found all that appealing.

5 THINGS TO TALK ABOUT INSTEAD OF YOUR KIDS

Perhaps you're so accustomed to talking about your grown-up kids at parties that you're afraid you won't have anything else to discuss. Here is a guide to some things to talk about besides your daughter's year abroad and your son's new house.

Instead of: 'My daughter's getting married in September.'
Say: 'Wow! Look at that hot guy over there!'

Instead of: 'My son's deciding between Oxford and Cambridge.'
Say: 'Don't you think this whole Oxbridge obsession is a bore?'

Instead of: 'My son is living in Japan.'
Say: 'Been on any great trips lately?'

Instead of: 'My daughter just got a big promotion. They love her, absolutely love her, at her company.'
Say: 'I'm thinking about changing careers. What would you do if you could do it all over again?'

Instead of: 'My daughter's about to have her first baby!'
Say: 'Don't you think sex is so much better now that you don't have to worry about getting pregnant?'

54 Don't Fear Rap

Rap music may seem like part of the plot by the evil young to drive us all to mass suicide so they can grab our high-paying jobs and steal our needlepoint pillows, but I'm here to tell you that you needn't be afraid of rap. After being tortured for countless hours in the car by rap music, I've even come to like some of it, though that might just be the Stockholm Syndrome talking.

True, the only rap music I actually like is the oldies. My number one favourite is the immortal Biggie Smalls singing 'Going Back to Cali' – he's heading west for 'the weather, the women, and the weed'. I like to quote it when I'm trying to get my fifteen-year-old son out of bed in the morning: 'Yo, Big, get your ass UP.' Though Biggie's been dead for more than a decade now, listening to him never fails to make me feel youngish. Another song (are they called songs?) I really like is Wu Tang Clan's 'C.R.E.A.M.', which stands for 'Cash Rules Everything Around Me', which sounds positively elderly. And then there's –

Well, that's about it for me. But if you want to impress your kids, consult the following guide to easy listenin' rap for some songs to download.

EASY LISTENIN' RAP: 9 SONGS EVEN YOU MIGHT LIKE

1. Soulja Boy: 'Crank Dat Dance'
2. Eminem: 'Cleanin' Out My Closet' (*awww*, what a good boy)
3. Lil' Kim: 'Ladies' Night'
4. Jay-Z: 'Hello Brooklyn 2.0'
5. Fat Joe: 'Lean Back'
6. Lupe Fiasco: 'Superstar'
7. Ludacris: 'Midnight Train'
8. Fabolous: 'Can't Deny It'
9. DMX: 'Lord Give Me a Sign'

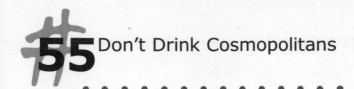

55 Don't Drink Cosmopolitans

I know they're delicious. I know they're fun. I know the 'girls' in the *SATC* movie tried their damnedest to help revive the Cosmo trend they launched when they were in their thirties.

Martinis may be back. Sidecars and Negronis may be back. The friggin' Pegu Cocktail may even be back.

But Cosmos have become the official cocktail of menopausal women. If you're a huge fan of the Cosmo, you can youngify it somewhat by turning it into a frozen drink: fresh-squeezed lime, a splash of cranberry juice, a little simple syrup, lots of vodka and ice in a blender. Mmmmm.

Or you could always knock back a vodka and Red Bull. Or order a so-old-it's-young-again drink like a Manhattan or a Mint Julep. Or try one of these lethal-sounding young cocktail recipes:

3 YOUNG COCKTAIL RECIPES

Kamikaze
Mix 2 oz vodka, 1 oz triple sec and 1 oz fresh lime juice. Shake all ingredients with ice and pour into old-fashioned glass with ice cubes.

Amaretto Sour
Mix 2 oz Amaretto, 1 oz simple syrup and 1 oz fresh lemon juice. Shake all ingredients with ice and strain into a sugar-rimmed glass. May be blended with ice for frozen drink.

Irish Car Bomb

Fill a shot glass with half Baileys Irish Cream (this goes on the bottom) and half Jameson Irish Whiskey. Pour a bottle of Guinness into a pint glass or beer mug until it's three-quarters full. Once the Guinness settles, drop the entire shot glass into the beer and down it. If you don't drink it fast enough, it will curdle and taste worse the longer you take to drink it.

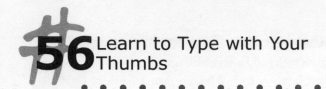

56 Learn to Type with Your Thumbs

Classic old people behaviour (of which I am guilty): dialling and typing on a phone with your index finger.

No no no no. You've got to pretend that your index finger doesn't even exist. Forget the middle, ring and pinky fingers, too.

The young way to dial your phone or to text or type on your BlackBerry or iPhone is with your thumbs. Yes, *exclusively* with your thumbs.

There are online guides to thumb typing, but I'm too impatient, and probably even too old, to read past Step 2 in the directions. Instead, I've been entertaining myself by typing away as fast as I can (not fast) with my thumbs on my new iPhone (yes! I'm so cool!) and then chuckling over the mistakes I make and how the iPhone corrects them.

Except sometimes the corrections are funnier than the mistakes. The other night I was trying to type 'there's no fucking way' – except what showed up on the screen was 'there's no ducking way'. So I typed it again, but this time with my index finger, checking like an old person to make sure I was hitting the right keys. That's when I saw that it was my iPhone that was automatically changing the 'fucking' to 'ducking'. Not so cool!

57 Cancel the Trip to Provence

Peter Mayle's *A Year in Provence* hit the bestseller list in 1991, whereupon every American who could afford it rented a villa in the south of France. If you figure that most of those people were at least thirty when they developed their passion for Provence, they're now nearly fifty. And like them, Provence is *peut-etre un peu* past its prime.

That's right: if you want not to act old, you've got to give up your fields of lavender, your striped hammocks, your country markets selling homegrown olives and artisanal wine. No more brightly printed table linens, buckets of sunflowers, espadrilles, or straw hats. The ancient *mas* with cornflower-blue shutters, vine-hung pergola and swimming pool must be traded in for someplace more *au courant*, youthful.

Like where, you may ask? Not, God forbid, Tuscany. That's just Provence with pasta. The Cotswolds and Cornwall, Umbria and the Dordogne are similarly played: the mojitos, the Burberrys of vacation destinations.

How about Berlin? Berlin is young, hip, happening. (I see you there, making a face, envisioning a grim grey city patrolled by scary guards in great coats. But that's an old image. Now Berlin is all emerging artists and musicians and cool lofts, or so I've heard. I have no desire to actually go there.)

Vietnam could work, or really anywhere that only old people remember as a war-torn wasteland: Croatia, Syria, Libya, Iraq – whoops, maybe not yet. We'll leave it to our children to sunbathe in Basra.

58 Edit the Anecdotes

• • • • • • • • • • • • • • • • •

I was riding in the car with my in-laws the other day when we passed a little take-away place that specializes in Southern food: fried chicken, sweet potatoes and corn bread.

'Oooh,' said my mother-in-law. 'Did we tell you about the time we went out to eat in Savannah and a storm blew out all the lights in the restaurant?'

Twenty minutes later, just as Mum was winding up this fascinating little story, we came to our destination and got out of the car, which reminded my father-in-law of the tale of buying his most recent Buick. And then, a bit after that, Mum told us the story about forgetting her tissues back at the house when she was packing her suitcase.

The point: The Greatest Generation is seriously attached to its anecdotes. Bring up any topic – dress shoes, say, or Coca-Cola, or the mating habits of bees – and your average septuagenarian will be reminded of a really great story that relates to it, however marginally.

The real point: edit your own compulsion to turn everything into a story. Sure, storytelling is the stuff of life. But anecdotes can easily start to sound like parables, which too often resemble sermons, which tend to put other people to sleep.

59 Don't Fear the Thong

All right, you know you're not supposed to wear granny panties. But what's wrong with bikinis? Why does acting young have to mean wearing a thong?

Thongs are . . . uncomfortable. Even the ones that are supposed to be comfortable are uncomfortable. They make you feel like you have an intractable wedgie. Plus, they make you feel completely exposed – like you're hardly wearing any underwear at all.

But listen, that's the next step: going commando, *à la* Britney. So think of thong-wearing as a compromise in sexiness.

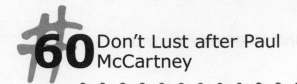

60 Don't Lust after Paul McCartney

Sigh. I know, I know. I used to love Paul, too. I lay on my bed with the radio pressed to my ear, singing along to 'I Want to Hold Your Hand'. Wooo! I wrote Paul a letter trying to persuade him that the difference in our ages and circumstances wouldn't and shouldn't stand in the way of our love. And when Linda died, I was sad, but also, my heart rose in hope, just a little bit.

I still kind of think Paul is cute, jowls and all, but admitting you think so will get you branded as old. Why? Because, as my daughter says, Paul McCartney is 'crusty'. Ew. Some male movie stars – think Sean Connery – can hold onto their sex appeal seemingly for ever, but poor Paul doesn't seem to be one of them.

But old guys aren't the only ones who can be crusty. Some younger guys can act or look like skeevy old ones and end up crusty, too. Here's the difference.

8 HOT VS. CRUSTY COMPARISONS

HOT	*vs.*	*CRUSTY*
Justin Timberlake		Paul McCartney
Jake Gyllenhaal		Ryan Philippe
Brad Pitt		Billy Bob Thornton
Will Smith		Willie Nelson
Daniel Craig		David Hasselhoff
Kiefer Sutherland		Marc Anthony
Clive Owen		Owen Wilson
George Clooney		George Bush

I'm sure you readers can think of female corollaries to this list, but I find it too depressing to do so myself.

No Chronic Health Discussions

. . . .

OK, if you're having a scary biopsy, or checking into the hospital, of course you should tell your family and closest friends. Yet as health issues multiply and other news in our lives recedes, it's too easy to tip over the line to Mabel and Ethel hunched in their rockers, one-upping each other on how many specialists they've seen, which symptoms they've suffered, and what gruesome tests and surgeries they've undergone.

See, even when you're old and sick and feel entitled to act like Mabel and Ethel, you shouldn't. So best practise reining it in now, before you start down that slippery slope. Can't order the cappuccino because you've recently worked out you're lactose intolerant? Just say 'No thank you' and move on. Chest still smarting from a particularly aggressive mammogram? Wear a cosy jumper and suck it up.

No one wants to hear about your hernia, your endometrial biopsy, your colonoscopy prep, your polyps, your heel spurs, your Botox injections, your periodontal treatment, your nice young gastroenterologist, your implants, your rosacea, your collapsed thumb joint, your bursitis, your neck wattle, your reflux, or your constipation. Anything I haven't mentioned, we don't want to hear about that, either.

#62 Screw the Housework

You get married, you buy a house, you have kids, and even if you keep working (obviously I'm talking to the women here), somehow it becomes all about the housework.

Here's what I mean: ask a fifty-two-year-old woman to describe her perfect man, and housework will creep into the description. He's great in bed, *and* he changes the sheets! He can cook you a great dinner, listen to you talk throughout the meal *and* happily cleans up afterward. Come to think of it, we can do without the sex and the conversation as long as he does the housework.

Think of your ideal life, and again housework inserts itself. You'd love a big, gorgeous house that cleans itself! Cosy family dinners without the dirty dishes. A beautiful wardrobe without laundry. Great parties with none of the shopping, cooking, or post-party swabbing.

'Well, of course,' I hear you saying. 'We know all too well what it takes to run a home and a life. These things don't just happen; they take work, effort, and you know who ends up doing it all! Of course we want a guy who knows his way around a vacuum!'

Yes, but . . . you didn't feel this way when you were twenty-two. 'I wish I had,' I hear you thinking. No, you don't really wish you had. You wanted to have sex and fun and wear cute clothes and go to yoga and listen to music and have a cool job, and not only is that okay for twenty-two, but it might improve the view from fifty-two as well. The problem with housework is that it takes so much time and energy that you don't have anything left over for creativity and the life of the mind. You spend all those years keeping a perfect house because you think people are going to judge you by it, and then suddenly the kids are grown up and you downsize to an apartment and you have no career and no hobbies and nothing interesting to talk about.

What? Oh, right. This is supposed to be funny. I nearly forgot.

MADLIBS: A YOUNG PERSON'S GUIDE TO HOUSEKEEPING

Old people make too big a deal of cleaning; it has to be done only every _____ days. You don't really need any special equipment,
<small>number</small>

just rags made from old _____ and lots of hot _____ in a
<small>clothing</small> <small>liquid</small>

big _____. It's best to start in the ____ which is usually the most
<small>container</small> <small>room</small>

_____ room in the house. Get down on your_____and begin
<small>adjective</small> <small>body part</small>

to____the _____. Next, ____ the _____. If you want, you can listen to
<small>verb</small> <small>noun</small> <small>verb</small> <small>noun</small>

some _____ while you work or even ask _____ to help you. You can
<small>sound</small> <small>person</small>

use a _____ to get the job done more _____. Don't worry
<small>household appliance</small> <small>adverb</small>

if there are a couple of _____ left in the corners; it doesn't have
<small>plural noun</small>

to be perfect. As long as all the _____ are put away and the place
<small>plural noun</small>

smells like _____, you'll feel _____. Pat yourself on the _____
<small>fragrance</small> <small>emotion</small> <small>body part</small>

, sit back and put up your feet, and enjoy a new kind of clean.

#63 Break that Saturday Night Sex Routine

I know what you do on Saturday nights. Or, if your kids are old enough to lie in, on Saturday or Sunday mornings. You have sex – or rather you fulfil your conjugal duty.

Let me just assure you that I agree there are lots of good reasons to corral sex into a regular, convenient time slot. I totally get (totally, dude) that Tuesday mornings are too rushed, Thursday nights you're too tired, that every other day is too often (it is, honey) – yet you can't let the frequency dwindle to once a month or you'd have to get d-i-v-o-r-c-e-d.

And yet, every-Saturday-night-whether-you-want-to-or-not sex has a way of making you not want to – has a way of reducing what once was fun and thrilling and satisfying and relationship-building to just another chore, like taking out the recycling on Monday morning. It's what you do when you're too old and/or you've been married too long to listen to your body instead of the calendar.

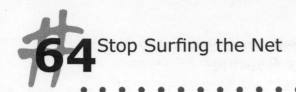

64 Stop Surfing the Net

If you still say you're 'surfing' the 'net', you've got to stop right now. I said RIGHT NOW! That phrase is just so 2003, or maybe 1998 – I don't know, all those years pretty much run together.

Don't spend any time in 'chat rooms', either. Or use the word 'cyberspace', except ironically.

In fact, if you want to get all modern about it, what you should do instead of surf is Tweet. I signed up for Twitter, apparently, and I've got reports that a couple of people are 'following' me, an activity whose dullness might be matched only by actually being me. What are you doing now? I'm typing. What are you doing now? I'm typing. What are you doing now? I'm still fucking typing, god-dammit!

The real point, though, is that web words have moved on.

25 WEB EXPRESSIONS YOU SHOULD KNOW NOW

Blackberry Thumb: malady resulting from overuse of one's handheld device.

Brain Fart: space out.

Cyber Monday: the Monday after Thanksgiving, aka the biggest online shopping day of the year.

Cyber Stalker: someone who stalks and harasses another person online.

Dead-tree Version: paper edition of a newspaper or book.

Ego Surfing: Googling yourself.

Fat Finger: typo excuse.

Flame War: heated online exchange.

Geeking Out: getting overinvolved in technology.

Impressions: number of times an online ad is seen.

Keyword: the word or phrase you use to search for something.

Link Farm: site that exists only to trade, sell and publish links.

Meatloaf: unsolicited personal e-mail.

Mommy Save: saving a computer file without first choosing a folder or directory.

Patch: supplemental code that fixes bugs.

Radio Button: small clickable circle on a web page.

Sandbox: limbo-like area to which new websites are consigned.

SEO (Search Engine Optimization): what websites do to try to come up higher on Google searches.

Troll: person who criticizes, baits, or attacks others online.

Tumblelog: a blog that's all pictures, links, quotes and videos, but no actual blog.

Vampire TIme: sleeping all day, staying up all night.

Voice Novel: endless voice mail.

Vubicle: cubicle with a view.

Wankware: online porn.

Widget: a graphic you put on your site containing HTML code that lets you access another website, database, or game.

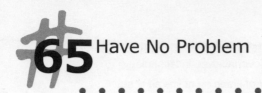

65 Have No Problem

When someone thanks you, how do you respond?

No, not by saying, 'You're welcome'. That's not only old-fashioned but is seen by young people as faintly hostile, as in 'You'd BETTER thank me, you selfish little snot-nose. Come to think of it, you should be licking my boots in gratitude.'

And you thought you were just saying the words Grandma taught you were polite.

Neither should you respond, 'My pleasure', even if you yourself find that phrase reassuring. It's also considered old-fashioned, and kind of servile, in the manner of your mum tripping all over herself to fix you your favourite snacks and do your laundry when you come to visit.

So what's left? 'No problem.' That's what the young say: 'No problem.' Or 'No worries', or 'No trouble.'

Though to my aging ears, I detect a note of hostility in *that*. I mean, why would you say 'No problem' unless there was the possibility of a problem in the first place? Sometimes, when I say thanks, it hasn't even vaguely occurred to me to worry about the favour that's been done for me – but if someone says, 'No worries', I immediately worry, 'Should I have been worried?'

Judging by how frequently they say it, though, young people have no 'No problem' problem.

66 Sponge off Your Parents

• • • • • • • • • • • • • • • •

With more 'kids' living longer than ever with their parents, why shouldn't you (in the interest of acting younger and dealing with the bad economy) join the trend? And it's not only a home you can sponge (or bum, leech, or scab) off Mum and Dad, but food, furniture, holidays, clothing and actual cash money.

Some useful things you can do with your time and money once Mum and Dad are footing the bill:

- Get an MA in poetry, explaining to your parents that this will eventually lead to a lucrative career in teaching other people to write poetry.

- Start a rock band, which will definitely make it big any day now.

- Invest in Marc Jacobs clothing, which will make you look amazingly cool for two months – at which point you'll have to throw it all out and start over.

- Become a rich and famous blogger, citing me as a role model.

If your parents are so elderly that they're dependent on you, or if they're uncool enough to have actually died, then your only hope is to try to get adopted by some nice elderly couple who will allow you to sponge off them in exchange for watching *Countdown* with them while you eat dinner and getting up on the ladder to clean out the gutters because you know Dad can't do that anymore. However, as an older orphan I tried to get adopted once, and I'm sorry to tell you that it didn't work out.

What if your grown-up kids are already sponging off you? Here's the plan: you *all* move in with *your* parents. Then, late at night, when Josh and Jess are out clubbing, and Mum and Dad are upstairs in a martini-and-Nurofen-induced haze, you sneak out, run as fast and far as you can, and leave no forwarding address. There comes a time when even the hardest-core *sponger* needs her independence.

67–73 How Not to Party Old

Not partying old doesn't mean you've got to regress to ordering a dozen pizzas and breaking out a keg. Just don't party ossified.

#67 Do Not Send 'Save the Date' Cards. That's like yelling 'shotgun' before you can see the car. Just because you show up with the invitation equivalent of an early bird special doesn't give you dibs on everybody's evening.

#68 No Pre-sunset Start Times. Unless you're serving tea at a nursing home, don't start the festivities at four or five or even six in the evening.

#69 Don't Serve Expensive Beef and Cheap Chardonnay. Old people usually get it the wrong way around: they spend days and weeks cooking the perfect food, then serve it with a couple of cheap bottles of warmish wine. The result: a bunch of people standing around feeling bloated, sluggish and way too sober. A far better party formula is perfectly icy martinis made with superlative spirits and a dish of stale crisps.

#70 Don't Spend a Week Polishing the House and No Time on Yourself. Don't slave away making your house look perfect and then dash upstairs and devote five minutes to getting yourself ready right before the party starts. Get your nails done! Have your hair blown out! Take a nap, for God's sake! Once the room's crowded, people are going to pay a lot more attention to you than to whether your pillows are lined up neatly.

#71 **No Bright Lights.** One of the top offenders at party of the old is glaring overhead lights – these not only expose every wrinkle but scream watch out! The grown-ups are here! Much better: candles everywhere.

#72 **No Soft Music.** OK, everybody wants to talk. But haven't all these people been talking to each other about the same boring fucking things for the past fifteen years? Mightn't they be ever so slightly relieved to find themselves drowned out by Marvin Gaye?

#73 **Don't End the Party before It Really Starts.** Don't troll around with a huge black plastic bag in your hands, throwing out everybody's glasses and napkins when they've barely got started. Relax, enjoy your own drinks and food, spend time with your guests and have at least as much fun as you want everyone else to have.

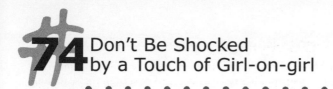

Don't Be Shocked by a Touch of Girl-on-girl

Hold onto your knickers, Grandma: lots of girls kiss other girls these days, and I'm not talking air kisses. And I mean straight girls. I mean very straight girls, such as pledged virgins who are looking to explore the boundaries of their sexuality without crossing over that thin pink line.

Cue oldster reminiscence: I remember when I first heard about the straight girl-on-girl phenomenon. I was at a writers' colony, working on my novel *Younger*, and left for the day to visit my twenty-something nieces Kimberly and Katie. Over dinner, I grilled them about what life was like for young women these days, and they told me about date-rape drugs, digital romance and dressing professionally in the age of Paris Hilton.

And then one of them said, very casually, 'Oh, and of course there's the thing about girls making out with other girls.' That's the point at which I spilled my Cosmo – my eyes popped out of my head and landed on the table. Yes, K & K informed me. It had become fairly standard for girlfriends to suck face (they didn't use that term; I heard it in *On Golden Pond*) as part of the evening's entertainment, to amuse onlooking guys as well as themselves.

Well, blow me down. When I went back to the writers' institution – I mean colony – and told this tale, the other middle-aged poetry scribblers were as shocked as I was. But a young woman who taught at a Southern college knew all about the new faux lesbians. 'All my female students do it,' she said. 'It's especially popular among the pledged virgins.'

I wrote it into the book, and I've been on the lookout for casual girl-on-girl action ever since, though it still doesn't seem to have hit my suburban New Jersey neighbourhood. But if you're in a bar in a city somewhere and you see two girls kissing passionately, don't be shocked or assume they're lesbians. And next time you're feeling affectionate towards another mum in your book group or your BFF, you might consider forgoing the peck on the cheek and slipping her a little tongue.

10 OTHER THINGS NOT TO BE SHOCKED BY

1. Threesomes
2. Gender-bending
3. Pierced anything
4. Oral sex not being considered sex
5. Casual profanity
6. Friends with benefits
7. No underwear
8. No hosiery
9. Babies before marriage
10. Obscene song lyrics

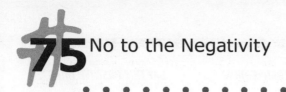# No to the Negativity

'It's all good', or so the young say. For you, that means you can never admit that sometimes it feels as if it's all bad, not even on the days when the drains back up and the teenager comes home high and you notice your first grey pubic hair.

The sad truth is that life can be more and more negative as you get older. That's because our bodies are falling apart and our parents are dying and our friends are getting cancer and our kids don't want to be with us and we haven't had hot new I-forgot-it-could-feel-like-this sex for, oh, twenty-three fucking years.

But who's complaining? Not you. If you have something bad to say – you know, any carping, complaining, criticizing – say it to another old person who speaks the same downer language. Or mutter it to yourself while shuffling along the street, poking at children and small animals with your cane.

Just don't say anything negative about, well, anything around a young person. If you're tempted to go to the dark side, simply say nothing, or consult this handy spin chart.

ANTI-NEGATIVITY SPIN CHART: 6 UPBEAT SUBSTITUTES

INSTEAD OF THIS NEGATIVE THING	*SAY THIS POSITIVE THING*
I'm so pissed off they fired me from that stupid job.	I feel blessed to have time at home with my family.
My teenager is driving me crazy.	We think Ethan would have better opportunities at boarding school.
If I have to eat one more meal sitting silently across the table from my spouse, I will scream.	I'm spending evenings at the yoga studio these days.
It's so frigging hot/cold/ rainy/nasty outside.	I just love to chill in the house.
I loathe you.	You're amazing, and yet, I've been lucky enough to meet somebody even more amazing.
I hate my hips.	I love my kneecaps.

76 Enough with the Man-bashing

Sad, isn't it? I mean, there go half my jokes – along with nearly all my fun.

That's right; it's time to retire those quips about male refrigerator blindness and brains in penises. But before we declare an absolute moratorium, let me just tell you my favourite man-bashing joke, first relayed to me by the divine Mave Maclean of Hampstead, London:

Q: What do you call the useless bit of flesh attached to a penis?
A: A man.

For those unregenerate man-bashers among you, there are plenty more great jokes out there.

But if you're determined to act younger, you should know that man-bashing has gone the way of bra-burning and do-it-yourself gynaecology – just another relic of old-style feminism. Feminists today love men, appreciate men, even revel in gender differences without needing to feel that men are in any way inferior to women, a stance I wholeheartedly support.

At least that's my story, and I'm sticking to it.

5 DEATHLESS MAN-BASHING JOKES

Psssst: these are the equivalent of the naughty postcards gentlemen used to pass around in the smoking parlour. Commit them to memory before they're outlawed:

Q: What do you call an intelligent, good-looking, sensitive man?
A: A rumour.

Q: What do you call a man with half a brain?
A: Gifted.

Q: Why did God create man?
A: Because a vibrator can't mow the lawn.

Q: What does it mean when a man is in bed gasping for breath and calling your name?
A: You're not holding the pillow down hard enough.

Q: What do you call a woman who knows where her husband is every night?
A: A widow.

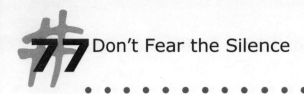

Don't Fear the Silence

Young people use silence to mean all kinds of things. I hate you, for instance. Or I'm not sure what to tell you, so I won't tell you anything. Or simply I'm busy, or I'm sleeping, or I'm distracted. It's hard to say, so I won't say anything.

If a young person important in your life – your adult child, say, or maybe your new boss – goes silent on you, try not to get nervous. Do not respond by chattering anxiously, leaving extended voice mails, or (the usual tactic of the old) sending several e-mails in a row. This will inevitably backfire, provoking even more silence.

Instead, chill. Wait till a text or e-mail comes in first, and then wait several hours – even overnight! – before responding. Make sure your reply contains fewer words than the original message: count if you have to. Don't get angry, just get silent.

What's that you say? This feels like high school? It's *all* high school, honey.

78 Don't Live Somewhere Old

The important thing here is the *perception* of the place. Clacton-on-Sea is most definitely old, Bournemouth is old, Bognor Regis and Dorset are OLD. So if you live in any of these places you have to move. Southampton is young, Exeter is young and London is most definitely young. Be careful about where in London you choose to put down roots though. The places where young people flocked when you were young are likely to be young no longer. Why? Money, honey. Young people want to live where it's cool, but they have to live where it's cheap, which forces them to move to places that are less cool, which makes these places more cool, which makes them more expensive, whereupon all the young, cool, poor people are forced to move even further out to the frontiers of civilization. So settle in Shoreditch or the East End, maybe Brixton – basically anywhere that makes you feel a little bit worried whilst walking about at night.

79 Don't Say the Doctor, the Copper, or the Teacher 'Looks Twelve'

• • • • • • • • • • • • • • • • • • • •

It's become a standard joke among old people to describe the authority figure they just encountered as being or looking twelve. Not eight. Not eighteen. Not thirty-two, which they (absurdly) figure is pretty close to their own advanced age, but eternally and inevitably twelve.

Besides losing its humorous edge, saying the doctor looks twelve really says that your point of reference has become alarmingly warped and you yourself look about a hundred and eight. Now *that's* funny.

80 Cancel the Dinner Party

• • • • • • • • • • • • • • • • • •

I didn't start throwing dinner parties until I was nearly forty. Too much work, too difficult to coordinate all those dishes – and who was going to take care of the kids while I shopped and cooked and cleaned and uncorked the wine and lit the candles and changed into a comfortable-yet-cleavage-baring dress and led the sparkling conversation?

And then, on our tenth wedding anniversary, I asked my husband what he'd change about me if he could, and he said he'd like it if I was able to give a nice dinner party. And so I learned. In fact, I got really good at it. Moving to the suburbs, living in a house with a real dining room, having more time on Saturday once our kids got older, we came to really enjoy dinner parties – giving as well as getting.

But now I think it's time to stop. I'm tired. Plus, they all start to feel the same. Now that I'm acting younger, I'm going to start inviting my friends over to share a keg and a bag of crisps – if they're really lucky, a pot of chilli – on Saturday nights.

81-87 How Not to Facebook Old

OK, so maybe you think you're oh-so-cool because you're on Facebook. You've even located your wall, joined a group or two and poked somebody. But if you're Facebooking old, you'd do better to stay home from the party. Here's what not to do on your friendly social network:

#81 No Formal Portraits. Is your official Facebook picture the one your company's HR department keeps on file? Is it the headshot from your book jacket, or maybe your official wedding picture? Oops, sorry, using any kind of posed, professional picture as your main Facebook photo is old. Your Facebook picture should be slightly tilted, somewhat blurry, and should feature you smiling but not like you think anyone's watching, designed to make the rest of the world envious of how totally awesome life can be, but only for you.

#82 Stifle the Oh-so-boring Status Updates. Joan is making stew in the slow cooker. Steve is turning in early tonight. Ruth is stuck in traffic again. Can you hear me yawning from there? We all know life is made up of such mundane moments, but you don't have to tell the world about them every single time one occurs. Young status updates are ironic and cryptic, and – here's a weird insider detail – they never erase the 'is'. So instead of 'Joe loves the TV show *Skins*', he'll write 'Joe is *Skins*'. What can I say? The young are strange.

#83 On the Other Hand, Remember that the World Is Reading. 'Susan really doesn't want to go to her stupid job today' and 'Dave just smoked a joint for the first time since college' are probably not messages you want to broadcast to everyone from the head of your office to your nephew 400 miles away.

#84 Don't Friend Your Non-friends. Acquaintances, okay. Colleagues and neighbours, sure. Long-lost cousins if you dare. But it really is not cool to use Facebook to do serious social climbing or business networking by trying to connect with people who would never be friends with you in real life. (And if you're on the receiving end, practise using that ignore button.)

#85 Know Where Your Wall Is. Remember when you started having sex and had no clue where the clitoris was? Don't let your ignorance of the placement of various central Facebook features drag on as long.

#86 Quit Sending All those Hugs and Trees. Facebook has dozens of apps you can send around to your friends, to give them a little love today or help save the planet. These are infinitely dorky and annoying.

#87 Don't Be Insulted If – When – Your Kids Defriend You. Now that the old are flocking to Facebook, the young are looking for another community, one with stronger gates. Until they defect *en masse*, recognize that ignoring your friend request or actively defriending you (you won't get a notice – you just won't be allowed onto their pages anymore) is not about you; it's about your age.

88 Crumble the Dried Flowers

• • • • • • • • • • • • • • • • • •

Nothing says you're desiccated like a bouquet of dried flowers — or five — arrayed about your living quarters. Dried flowers are the antimacassars, the china figurines of today. Doesn't matter whether they're hydrangeas from your own garden (you have a garden?), ornamental grasses you gathered yourself, or blossoms fashioned into swags and wreaths: dried flowers are the decorating accent of the middle-aged.

What kind of flowers should you display instead? Not, God forbid, plastic. Silk are nearly as bad. Even potted plants are a tad fiftyish.

Can fresh flowers ever be wrong? They can if you leave the baby's breath and florists' greenery in the arrangement. Or if the bouquet is turning brown or drooping: pathetically symbolic. But for the most part, okay, fresh flowers are lovely and ageless.

89 Forget the Sixties Nostalgia

● ● ● ● ● ● ● ● ● ● ● ● ● ● ● ● ● ●

So, you were at Woodstock? Ate mushrooms with Kesey, chanted with Ram Dass, wrote poetry naked with Ginsberg?

I'm sure that was all mind-blowingly groovy, but I have news for you, Grandpa (and Grandma): reminiscing about the sixties now is like recalling Prohibition was when we were young. Cue wavering voice: 'Let me tell you, sonny, we got up to some crazy shenanigans in those speakeasies.' For those of you who are mathematically challenged, it's been forty whole years since 1969.

As further illustration of how long ago that all was, check out these words coined in 1929, forty years before 1969, from the Online Etymology Dictionary: beep, jeepers, deep six. But terms brought to you by 1969 don't sound much more modern: doo-wop, singles bar and ego trip.

The point: the sixties are ancient history and not of great interest to anyone who wasn't actually there. So too the seventies: we really don't need to know who did what to whom that night you went to Plato's Retreat (ewwww, you did?) or what you snorted with whom at Studio 54. Even the eighties, which I basically missed thanks to the joys of parenthood, are getting kind of antique.

Young people are allowed to have nostalgia for the decades and icons of their childhoods: early Madonna and late Kurt Cobain, leg warmers and flannel shirts. You can reminisce about where you were in Y2K.

90 Don't Wake Up Before Dawn

Getting up when it's still dark outside is what Seinfeld's parents did. Remember? Jerry goes to visit and is awakened in the dark to find his parents in the kitchen making coffee and squeezing juice. 'We thought we'd let you sleep in,' they say. To which he responds, aghast, 'It's 5:30 in the morning!'

Ahem.

I was up at six today, Sunday morning. And that's after going to bed at almost eleven! Even when I stay up really late – till midnight – I wake up at six.

I blame my children, for making me wake up at or before dawn for all those years to nurse them or watch cartoons with them or drive them to school. Now, although they ridicule me for waking up early, I can't stop. But at least I'm conscious enough to know it's an old people thing.

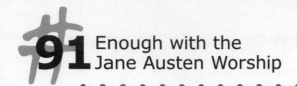

91 Enough with the Jane Austen Worship

I like Jane Austen as much as the next novel-writing and -reading middle-aged woman, which is to say a lot. Which is really to say way, way too much.

Do we actually need a whole genre of books about modern Jane Austen lovers, entire clothing lines devoted to Jane Austen gear, multiple tour companies eager to guide you through Jane Austen locales? How about lessons in how to take tea, dance, cook, garden and, of course, write *à la* Jane Austen? There are Jane Austen Festivals and Jane Austen book groups, Jane Austen dolls and Jane Austen T-shirts, Jane Austen movies and Jane Austen bloggers.

Even our babies are not exempt from Jane's influence; the names Emma, Darcy and, yes, Austen are rising in popularity. And once those little Austens get older, they can play with their very own Jane Austen action figures.

It's not that Jane hasn't written some great books, but there's something a little too order-seeking, rich-man-loving and sanitized (i.e., fussily middle-aged) about the JA mania. Why not devote equal attention to the Brontës, who pulled back the curtain on a wilder brand of early womanhood? Or to modern masters of our own generation like Alice Munro or Louise Erdrich who are far less widely known and sell many fewer books than Jane Austen?

Listen, I love *Pride and Prejudice*, but I'd rather support contemporary female novelists whose talents are in more danger of being lost and forgotten.

15 COOL DEAD FAMOUS PEOPLE

1. **Abraham Lincoln**
2. **Princess Diana**
3. **JFK Jr.**
4. **MLK Jr.**
5. **Heath Ledger**
6. **Michael Jackson**
7. **Jimi Hendrix**
8. **Audrey Hepburn**
9. **John Lennon**
10. **Ted Kennedy**
11. **Farrah Fawcett**
12. **Wolfgang Amadeus Mozart**
13. **James Dean**
14. **Coco Chanel**
15. **Kurt Cobain**

8 UNCOOL DEAD FAMOUS PEOPLE

1. **Richard Nixon**
2. **Madame Chiang Kai-Shek**
3. **John Wayne**
4. **Wicked Witch of the West**
5. **Keith Floyd**
6. **Rudyard Kipling**
7. **Mata Hari**
8. **Jade Goody**

92 Don't Fear the Remote

There's a moment in the life of all children when (if you and they are lucky) they leave you, not only physically but psychically – when their attention turns from you to the larger world, and when they become certain that they'll be happier seeking their fortune Out There than staying home with Mummy and Daddy.

That moment, for our older son, happened the night we called him at a party to help us change the channel on our TV. Until then, he'd always been around to work the remote, or we'd managed to muddle through without him. But that night we wanted to tune to On Demand, and no amount of fiddling could get us there, and so we finally broke down and interrupted Joe at his loud, beer-soaked soiree.

Right then and there, I think, Joe decided that he had to break free of the tyranny of our unreasonable requests or we would swallow him whole. And we found ourselves having to learn to work our own remote.

I'm not saying it's easy. Or that we've ever got very good at it. But we do now know when we need to be on AV-1 instead of terrestrial and how to get there. We know how to Sky+ one show and watch another. We're even capable of double-remoting ourselves from conventional to On Demand television.

Best of all, we no longer fear our remote. Instead, we fear our son.

93 No History

History, don't you know, is for old people. If it happened before, say, 2001, who really cares? Nostalgia, revivals, historical tomes, national monuments, museums, antique stores, restored villages and please, dear God, re-enactments of any kind, just plain suck.

The reason history is for the old is that it makes them feel (erroneously) that there's something interesting and valuable about things that took place a long time ago, such as their lives. But there's not.

So let the old books crumble into dust. Tear up the mobcaps and throw the muskets in the fire. Ignore the historic marker, blow off the museum and head to the bar.

If you want to not act old, you've got to live for today, forget the past and believe – since you have no evidence to the contrary – that everything will be better tomorrow.

94 Don't Plan

When old people want to go on holiday to, say, Italy next summer, what do they do? They buy tickets. Book a hotel. Research restaurants and make reservations. They plan, in other words, just like they plan dinner parties for three weeks from Saturday, buy theatre tickets for Christmas, and make a mammogram appointment for the following April.

If you want not to act old, you've got to be a little looser than that – nay, a lot looser. Decide what you're going to do on the spur of the moment, depending on how you feel. Make travel arrangements on the go. Throw out your calendars and diaries. Be here now.

95 Don't Be Named Bob or Pat

• • • • • • • • • • • • • • •

Or Pam or, God forbid, Dick. There's a whole generation of names last popular in the forties and fifties – Karen and Donald, Barbara and Leonard – that you've got to avoid if you don't want to seem old.

Of course, you didn't choose your own name and you're pretty much stuck with it, unless you want to do something really radical and change it to one that sounds young: Josh or Jessica, if you want to go thirtyish. But those names are aging fast, so you may want to go even younger, with a name like Justice or Jagger. Or turn the whole age-name thing on its head and pick a really old name that's popular for babies: Matilda, say, or even Moses.

CHANGE YOUR NAME/CHANGE YOUR AGE:
10 UPDATES FOR YOUR OLD FART NAME

Use this handy chart to convert your old person's name to a younger model. For a subtle change, go slightly younger – or go all the way to childlike!

REGULAR OLD NAME	10 YEARS YOUNGER	30 YEARS YOUNGER
Judy	Jody	Jolie
Ken	Kent	Kendall
Mary	Mariah	Mackenzie
Wayne	Blaine	Zane
Carol	Holly	Christmas
Bill	Will	Willow
Kathy	Katie	Kaydee
Carl	Charley	Carlo
Elaine	Elena	Delaney
Dick	Rick	Brock

96 Torch Your Books

Here is one of the many ways that I can't – nay, won't! – stop acting old. I refuse to stop reading. I even insist on reading some things printed on actual paper (aka papyrus scrolls) and not containing four-colour pictures.

People in my age and gender group – fiftyish women – are found in studies to be the most likely to read books, while our male counterparts are the only ones left reading newspapers. Young women are paging through celebrity mags and reading vampire romance graphic novels, while young males are playing *Grand Theft Auto* or looking at internet porn instead.

If you're not about to trade in *Anna Karenina* for Niko Bellic (if you don't know who that is, ask your teenage son), you may want to revisit your youth by reading Meg Cabot's *Forever Princess*, to remember when you thought love would solve everything; Erica Jong's *Fear of Flying*, to remember why you started having sex with everybody you could get your hands on; Sue Miller's *The Good Mother*, to remember why you stopped; and Sheila Weller's *Girls Like Us*, to remember the women you wished you were (and are ultimately glad you're not).

7 WAYS TO READ YOUNGER

OLD READING MATERIAL	*YOUNG READING MATERIAL*
Newspapers	Blogs
Historical romances	Vampire romances
Mysteries	Graphic novels
GQ	*Game Informer*
Stephen King	*Harry Potter*
The Grapes of Wrath	*Wicked*
O, The Oprah Magazine	*Cosmopolitan*

97 Get off the Eternal Diet

• • • • • • • • • • • • • • • • • • • •

I hate to say it, but I tend to be perennially on a diet, rarely at the weight I want to stay. Tedious, frustrating and old, old, old.

Why old, and not merely fat? Because it lacks the can-do spirit evidenced by younger women. That 'better body after baby' ideal, that *Biggest Loser* mentality. It was our mothers and their friends who were always trudging to Weight Watchers, yet never quite managing to be thin.

Of course, if you're not always on a diet, you might get even fatter. But at least you won't be so old.

YOUNG PERSON'S DIET AND EXERCISE PLAN: 13 SIMPLE STEPS TO NEVER GAINING AN OUNCE

7 a.m.: Run five miles

7:40 a.m.: Have amazing sex

8:37 a.m.: Grab superdouble grande latte on way to work.

9 a.m. till noon: Drink two more pots of coffee.

12:30 p.m.: Eat Nutri-Grain bar and cake left over from yesterday's office party.

1 p.m.: Stand shivering in cold while smoking cigarettes with cute co-worker.

3 p.m.–5 p.m.: Drink Diet Coke and eat large bag of chips.

6 p.m.: Yogalates.

7:30 p.m.: Meet friend for drinks: three frozen mojitos and twelve cigarettes.

9 p.m.: Starving for dinner. Eat four rolls, two shrimp, and one pepper slice.

11 p.m.: Eat bowl of Crunchy Nut Cornflakes with sugar while checking e-mail.

Midnight: Have more amazing sex.

Sleep a few hours and do it all again.

 **Say Yay!**

• • • • • • • • • • • • • • • • • • • •

Happy? Excited? Managed to uncork the champagne, find a pair of Louboutins on sale in your size, land the job?

Here's what you say: yay! Not loudly and energetically, like you're a cheerleader at a football game. But softly and, well, coolly, with perhaps a little twist of your head. Yay! Be sure to infuse the word with a touch of irony but an equal measure of sincerity. You're happy. You know it. But you're way too cool to get embarrassingly carried away.

If the news is *really* amazing – let's say Ryan Reynolds leaves Scarlett Johansson for you, or you win a reality show – you may accompany your yay with a little Snoopyesque happy dance. A little one, I said: cute and never out of control.

Yelps, tears, 'Oh, My God!'s, and other over-the-top expressions of joy are for the tacky and the old.

#99–124 How Not to Holiday Old

People say that one of the best things about getting older is that you finally have the time and freedom to travel. Except when you actually get older, it becomes a lot more difficult – psychologically, I mean, not canes and walkers difficult – to get yourself out of the house and on the road.

Here's how to transcend the travelling challenges that come with age:

Before You Go:

#99 Do Not Book Your Flights, Arrange Your Accommodations, or Plan Your Itinerary So Far Ahead that when the date gets near, you can no longer remember what airline you're flying on, what time you're leaving, or even exactly where you're going.

#100 Resist the Temptation to Panic and Pack Your Entire Life. You don't need six pairs of shoes, clothing for every weather possibility from heat wave to gale-force blizzard, plus your special coffee and the pillow that keeps your spouse from snoring.

#101 No Luggage Too Heavy for You to Actually Lift.

#102 . . . and No Luggage that Matches. Unless it's Vuitton.

#103 And **No Bum Bags.** Even – make that especially – Vuitton.

#104 If you ignore my advice about packing light, at least **Don't Bring Everything from Your Back-up Trainers to Three Purple Jumpers and Then Forget Your Life-saving Medication.**

#105 Don't Leave Your Plumber's Phone Number and Your Life Insurance Policy with Your Neighbour 'just in case'.

#106 Speaking of 'just in case', **You Don't Need to Wash the Last Sock in Your Eternal Laundry Pile and Pay All Your Bills before You Leave.** You are coming back – if you can ever actually get out of the house in the first place.

#107 Don't Travel an Entire Three Miles from Home Only to Have to Turn around Because You Think You Might Have Left the Iron On. (Why do you have an iron?) Or because you think you might not have locked the door. Or because you have to go to the bathroom.

If You're Flying:

#108 Do Not Get to the Airport Three and a Half Hours Ahead of Time. Yes, it takes a while to get through security these days: maybe seventeen minutes. Then you've still got a whole three hours and thirteen minutes to kill, and there are only so many pretzels a person can eat.

#109 **Do Not Dress Up for the Flight.** Assuming you're neither the pilot nor a flight attendant, there is no need to wear a tie, skirt, hat with a shiny visor, shoes more formal than flip-flops, or a bra. If you feel sloppy, you can always add epaulets with gold stars to your pyjamas.

#110 **Don't Make Friends** with the person sitting next to you. Unless it's ScarJo. (That's Scarlett Johansson for you oldies.)

If You're Driving:

#111 **Don't Travel Five Miles off the Motorway in Search of Petrol that's Five Pence a Gallon Less.** Modern maths: the seventy-five pence you save won't even buy you a can of coke.

#112 **No Scenic Routes.** Scenic routes, with their cows and their small towns, their speed traps and their no-passing zones, are old – and they're often not even that scenic anymore.

#113 If you get lost and have to pull into a petrol station to ask for directions, **Don't Keep Nodding as If You Totally Understand and Then Turn the Wrong Way** right out of the car park. Not that you've ever done that, honey.

Accommodations:

#114 **Do Not Stay at One of those Guesthouses that Smell Like Air Freshener** and offer an assortment of herbal teas and have little signs posted everywhere that say things like 'Thank you for removing your make-up before putting your head on the pillow!' You know, those signs that make you want to go out and buy some make-up just so you can rub foundation into the pillow.

#115 If You Stay at a Travelodge Instead of One of those Guesthouses, Don't Say You Have a Nice Room. They're all nice. They're all identical.

#116 Don't Rent a House and Car Exactly Like the house and car you have at home.

Once You're There:

#117 Don't Spend More Time Putting on Sunblock than you spend in the sun.

#118 Forget Shopping. You already brought too much stuff in your giant suitcase.

#119 Don't Be the First One in the Restaurant at breakfast – not to mention dinner.

#120 No Guided Tours. In Fact, No Tourism. You're a traveller. No, you're practically a native! If you see a tourist or a tour, act appropriately scornful.

#121 Don't Be Afraid to Go Somewhere Brand New. They will definitely have bathrooms there – plus some kind of food that doesn't upset your stomach.

#122 **Don't Over-worry about the Weather.** Go on holiday like the young do. If it rains, have sex. If it's too cold to go to the beach, have sex. Even if it's nice outside, have sex.

#123 **If You're Travelling Alone and End Up Having Sex with a Stranger, Don't Imagine that You're Ever Going to See Him or Her Again.** But don't feel guilty about it, either. If you're travelling with your spouse and end up having sex with a stranger, you should of course feel guilty. But way not to act old, dude or dudette!

When You're Back Home:

#124 **Don't Claim that Now You Need Another Holiday.** That's not just old, it's obnoxious!

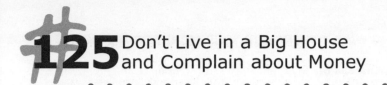

125 Don't Live in a Big House and Complain about Money

We get it that maybe you bought your house a couple of booms ago when prices were low, so you're really not as rich as you look. We understand that the taxes on a house that big are through the roof (so to speak), and you don't even want to think about what your heating bill is going to be this year.

And to all that we say: oh, boo hoo.

If you're lucky and old enough to live in a big house or a sprawling apartment you bought in 1986 for £20,000, you're not allowed to complain. Yes, even if you've got cash-flow problems – even if you're only halfway through putting the second kid through college. If you need money so badly, sell the house and move into the kind of place you can buy for £20,000 these days: a campervan.

6 WAYS TO RENOVATE YOUR MONEY COMPLAINTS

Instead of: 'My council taxes just went up again.'
Say: 'I could have saved the tax on that pair of Louboutins by having them shipped to my parents' house, but the humiliation wasn't worth it.'

Instead of: 'I had to work all last night balancing my chequebook.'
Say: 'I don't think I ever got a chequebook.'

Instead of: 'My kids' tuition is going up again.'
Say: 'My parents don't have a right to see my grades just because they pay my tuition.'

Instead of: 'Can you believe how much a Chanel bag costs these days?'
Say: 'A Chanel bag is worth it because it makes everyone take you seriously.'

Instead of: 'Can you believe how much David Beckham made last year?'
Say: 'If I only had a thousand pounds, I could stop worrying about money.'

Instead of: 'I had to pay £3.99 for mustard.'
Say: 'Isn't mustard, like, free?'

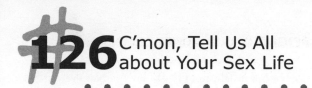

#126 C'mon, Tell Us All about Your Sex Life

How often do you have sex? Do you have orgasms? Only when you masturbate, or during intercourse, too? What exactly makes you come? How do you move, what do you think about, how long does it take?

What? What's that you say? That information is too personal? Well, you must be over forty.

Which details about your sex life you're willing to divulge to whom varies greatly depending on how old you are, a study conducted solely in my head shows. Here, my findings by age:

Under 21: Happily share half-naked pictures of self and divulge all details of hook-ups – who, what, how big, how good, etc. – with several hundred Facebook 'friends'. At least that's my fear.

21–30: No shame about strutting around naked at the gym or lifting up a shirt to display boobs at party. Will freely discuss all aspects of sex life – including details on partners, habits and problems – with friends, colleagues, and random strangers they encounter at a meet-up. (What's a meet-up? That's another discussion.)

30–40: Will openly talk about everything from orgasms to waxing habits to porn viewership with anyone they've met more than, say, once.

40–50: Most follow the *Sex and the City* model, sharing intimate details with close friends but otherwise keeping it quiet.

50–60: People in their fifties, who came of age during the Sexual Revolution, may be open enough to experiment with sex toys, positions and fantasies – but usually not to talk about it. Not even with their closest friends. Maybe not even with the person they're doing it with.

60 plus: The door is firmly shut, and they've thrown away the key.

127 Scratch that Golf Game

Some sports are young, and some sports are old. Examples?

Basketball is young; baseball is old.

Snowboarding is young; skiing is old.

Skateboarding is young; roller-skating is old.

And golf is old. So old I can't even think of something similar-yet-different (miniature golf? No. Croquet? Nah.) to put on the young side of the equation.

Why? It's expensive, for one thing. It's slow; not all that strenuous; the outfits are not very cute. And the shoes!

Plus, golf takes planning – you need to reserve the course days, weeks, or even years in advance. And it takes patience, a quality that tends to increase with age.

The only thing about golf that has any youth appeal are the buggies. I would like to ride around a golf course in one of those buggies. I just don't want to have to wear shoes with cleats or knock any little balls out of the sand.

128 Never Admit You Have No Freaking Clue Who Leighton, Dappy, Rihanna, Little Boots, Tinchy, or Pixie Are

• • • • • • • • • • • • • • • • • • •

They all swim together, these strangely named, androgynous-sounding, ethnically ambiguous young stars. Does Pixie work for Father Christmas? Is Tinchy very small? A boy or a girl? Does Little Boots actually wear small shoes? And does Dappy describe a state of mind? Is Leighton male, female, or both?

Quiz time!

Pair the twelve names below into first and last and then match the person you've created with an occupation. Bonus points for correctly identifying gender.

Names
A. Leighton
B. Little Boots
C. Dappy
D. Tinchy
E. Rihanna
F. Pixie
G. Robyn
H. Lott
I. Meester
J. aka Victoria Hesketh
K. aka Dino Contostavlos
L. Stryder

Occupations
1. Teenage singing sensation
2. An N-Dub
3. Gossip Girl
4. A London rapper
5. Barbadian pop singer
6. Electropop singer-songwriter who had success with *Remedy*

And the answers are:

1. **Leighton Meester** is one of the (female) stars of *Gossip Girl*, a show that your teenager undoubtedly loves because the characters have as much money and sex as adults (more!) with none of the icky responsibility.

2. **Dappy**, aka Dino Contostavlos, one member of N-Dubz – a MOBO award winning hip hop group from Camden town.

3. **Robyn Rihanna**, who also goes by her last name only, is a Barbadian pop singer and Grammy winner who looks amazing in sparkly dresses.

4. **Little Boots**, aka Victoria Hesketh, is an electropop singer-songwriter. The name Little Boots is in fact a reference to her very small feet.

5. **Tinchy Stryder** is a London-based rapper whose friends include Wiley and Dizzee Rascal.

6. **Pixie Lott** is a Brit Award nominated teenage singer-songwriter and actress.

129 Turn Your Stereo Up and Your TV Down

Why do our senses get selectively better or worse as we get older? Suddenly we can't hear the television at all, and have to keep pumping up the volume until we all but blast younger folk out of the room. Yet at the same time, music any louder than a lullaby is painful to our ears.

It's been forty years since I took any kind of science class – and I think I got a D in that one – but empirically this evidence would seem to suggest that the problem is not really in our hearing *per se,* but in our sensibilities. So one solution might be to pay closer attention to what the people are saying on television, and at the same time turn up the music the way you did when you were twenty-two.

Of course, it's also possible that all the loud music we listened to in our youth has actually made us deaf, and that at the same time we've become crankier.

130 Unless You're in Nagasaki, Don't Give (or Ask for) Directions

● ● ● ● ● ● ● ● ● ● ● ● ● ● ● ● ● ● ●

Once, when I was looking for a swimming hole in Maine, a local told me to turn left where the old school burned down. That's what giving directions is like these days. In this era of Mapquest and GPS, it's meaningless to tell someone to turn left at the church, go under the railroad trestle and look for the yellow house.

Let the computer do the work for you. If the other person gets lost, blame it on their digital guide. When we all have chips implanted in our brains, we'll never again have any need to know where we are or where we're going; we'll just go wherever Google tells us.

131 No Hovering

Dear Marge,

I realize that, in the 396 public toilets I've visited in the past week on the road, someone else might have been the culprit. But the fact is, the only one I really suspect is you.

I know your mum told you that sitting on the seat of a public toilet could give you a disease. Mummy watched to make sure you hovered over the toilet without letting anything touch anything else. Ever since, you've found it impossible to allow yourself to actually sit down on a public toilet, so instead you pee half-standing up.

But your aging thighs aren't up to holding you steady, so guess what, Marge: you sprinkle the seat. You flush and leave, and when I enter the stall, there is your pee left all over for ME to sit in. Or clean up. Maybe you feel all clean and smug and satisfied because YOU avoided sitting on the public toilet seat. But did you ever stop to think about what you're doing to me?

#132 Don't Cook the Roast

It's an unwritten law of the universe: no one under the age of forty knows how to cook a roast. No one under the age of forty *wants* to know how to cook a roast. A roast symbolizes childhood Sundays, dinner with the relatives and leftovers. Besides, cooking the roast is *Mum's* job, not ours.

And then, at some point in middle age, most of us realize that a roast is not only delicious and substantial but just about the easiest thing to cook. Eight for dinner? Twelve for Christmas? Sixty for an open house? All you need is a meat thermometer and a giant hunk of beef, pork, or lamb, and dinner's done.

It's guaranteed that your younger friends and relatives will be grateful, not to mention awed, that you cooked that magnificent roast. But they won't respect you for it. Instead, they'll assign you a permanent apron, a grey bun and a pair of rimless spectacles plastered to the tip of your oven-scorched nose.

12 STEPS TO MAKING DINNER YOUNG

Pour yourself a large glass of wine. Swearing that you waste time and money going out to dinner or ordering a takeaway every night, make up your mind to cook.

Select **a lively playlist** to keep you company.

Open a **bag of crisps.** It's not smart to cook on an empty stomach. Or is that shop?

Go to a recipe site – recipematcher.com is one – that helps you work out what you can cook based on what's in your refrigerator. Let's see: gnocchi from the restaurant the other night, a half carton of olives and some mouldy strawberries. **We got nothin'.**

In order to do a **proper food shop**, you'd have to buy a car and move to the suburbs, a considerably more expensive enterprise than ordering a takeaway. Pour yourself another glass of wine.

Wish you were one of those worldly people who could conjure dinner from thin air. A little oil, a little garlic, a little pasta . . .

Hey, you have **oil, garlic and pasta!** Heat oil, peel garlic, boil water for pasta, feeling pretty damn worldly after all.

Multitask by checking BlackBerry while water boils. You're so domestic, you're so adept; you might be ready to have a baby after all!

Ooops, **work emergency!** By the time you clear it, garlic has fried to nothing and pot has boiled itself black.

Significant other arrives home to find you in tears. A few kisses and hugs later, feel not only comforted but distinctly amorous. Forgetting hunger, make love.

A few hours later, **stomachs growling,** revisit the dinner situation. Options: Manny's Indian Takeaway (again) or Maria's Corner Trattoria (again). But you swore you were going to make dinner yourself!

Solution: one jar of peanut butter. Two spoons.

133 Don't Lust after the Lifeguard

When you were thirteen, you had the hugest crush on the lifeguard who totally ignored you. Then, when you were nineteen or twenty-three, the lifeguard may have lusted after you – but you decided he was too shallow to warrant your attention. When you were thirty-five, you were too busy making sure the kids didn't drown to notice him.

It's only now that you're able to fully appreciate the lifeguard's virtues, and to fantasize that maybe he appreciates yours in return. This is the point at which you have to imagine me slapping you across the face and crying, 'Snap out of it!'

Unless we're talking about the world's Oldest Living Lifeguard – you know, the one whose skin is so weathered you could make a bag out of it – the lifeguard is too young for you.

10 SIGNS YOU MIGHT BE A LECH

1. You think the babysitter is hot for you.

2. Your favourite romantic screen couple is Woody Allen and Mariel Hemingway in *Manhattan*.

3. When your assistant compliments your shoes, you think she means it.

4. You skip the game, but watch the halftime show.

5. You really think the Monica Lewinsky thing was unfair to Bill.

6. That time you drove a convertible, you thought everyone was looking at you – I mean, looking at you favourably.

7. You have your own subscription to *Glamour*.

8. You comb over.

9. You flirt with the counter girl at McDonald's.

10. You think your son's girlfriend likes him because he looks like you.

134 Dehyphenate Your Name

There was a brief moment when name hyphenization seemed like the answer to all marital equality issues. A moment when two people might have got married and become Pamela and Richard Redmond-Satran. (Not that we did that: my husband declined to take the Redmond, so I just dragged both names behind me like a big fat butt, without even a hyphen to connect them.)

But back to you: the whole hyphen thing seemed like a good idea for about a minute and a half, until the jokes started about what would happen when Gabriella Redmond-Satran (not one of our real children) married Marmaduke Martini-O'Flaherty. Would their child be called Maximilian Redmond-Satran-Martini-O'Flaherty?

And then there was the question of whose name went first, and whether the husband as well as the wife would adopt the hyphen, until the notion just collapsed. Before that happened, however, several hundred people got married and hyphenated their names. All those people are now over the age of fifty – or just sound like it.

#135 Don't Fear the Teenager

Let's face it: teenagers are frightening. They sleep till dusk, wallow in filth, spend much of their time steeped in electronic violence and pornography, and the rest of their time getting high and squandering your money. They drive too fast, have irresponsible sex, take insanely dangerous risks and – scariest of all – are perversely adept at making us feel ancient.

If confronted by a teenager, try not to show your fear. Do not talk loudly in an artificially cheerful voice. Do not ask such inane questions as 'How's school?' or 'Where do you want to go to college?' Do not, for the love of God, attempt to 'get down' with the teen by mimicking adolescent slang or mannerisms.

Instead, back slowly away, taking care to make no sudden noises. Open your wallet and hand over several thousand pounds to a university, any university, that will take the teen off your hands. With any luck, you'll get your scary teenager back in three (or maybe four) years, repackaged as an adult.

136 Stop Bossing Everybody Around

So you think you know it all, do you? Think you're so on top of everything that you know what everybody else should be doing – and don't hesitate to tell them?

I've seen this phenomenon before, on the first few seasons of *Survivor*. It was always the older competitors who thought they had such superior experience in hut-building, berry-picking and fish-spearing that they could organize the whole camp and tell everyone what to do, and that that would make their teammates respect and value them.

And guess what happened? That's right: they were voted off. The young hotties would sit there and smile and nod and then go to tribal council and *zap*. So you be a smiler and a nodder, too, and the boss of only yourself.

#137 Don't Send Greetings Cards

Remember when your grandmother would send you a birthday card with a tenner inside as a present? That's what it still feels like when you send someone a greetings card: like it came from Grandma.

You can update the experience by making your own card (make sure it looks aggressively handmade, like something you'd see on etsy.com), sending a vintage postcard, or using one of those blank cards with the funny pictures that are trying so hard to be cool. But I'm afraid greetings cards are one of those niceties of life that are going the way of the paper invitation.

138 No Matching Anything

Matching marks you as belonging to an earlier time and sensibility, when all things had to be tidily coordinated and anyone who was sane and solvent bought everything from their jewellery to their living-room furniture to their luggage to their bathroom accessories – down to the toilet-paper-roll covers – in complete sets.

This is an aesthetic that went out with matching cashmere jumpers and kneesocks. Yet – perhaps influenced by catalogue retailers, who have an interest in making you feel as if you need to buy the chair and the end table and the rug and the pillows that go with the sofa as pictured – overmatching lives on. But matched anything belies a certain insecurity, a lack of imagination, that can make you seem stodgy and old-fashioned and just plain old.

So go ahead, unmatch. Wear silver with gold, brown with black, suede with patent. Put Grandma's Victorian armchair next to your Ikea sofa; sling an Anya Hindmarch handbag over your shoulder and lug your shopping home in an Asda bag-for-life. The less you match, the freer you'll feel – and the younger you'll seem.

#139–143 U Can't Has Convertible

When you're young, you see these geezers zooming around in these hot little convertibles, sparse wisps of grey hair whipping in the breeze, and you think, Jesus, that old dude looks so fucking ridiculous. I am going to remember this moment and I am never, ever, no matter what, going to let myself buy a convertible when I get old and pathetic.

And then you hit some ancient birthday, and the kids have left home liberating you from the minivan, and you've got a little money in your pocket, and you think, Now I can finally buy myself a convertible.

But then you remember that moment when you were young, and how you promised yourself that you would never be that decrepit guy in the convertible. Except you're not that decrepit, are you? Your face is not that wizened, your bald spot not that shiny, your presence behind the wheel of a convertible not that absurd, correct?

Incorrect. Now that you have a life and a budget that can actually accommodate a convertible, you can't actually have one or you risk committing a crime against style and decency. And if you claim you don't care about any of that, if you go ahead and buy a red Boxster anyway, all I can say is that you're never going to be able to unselfconsciously enjoy it.

#139 Don't Name Your Car. It's not funny and it's not clever and it will just make you seem old. Calling your car 'Tilly' or 'Bessie' or 'Hootie' is just not cool.

#140 No 'Ironic' Nodding Dogs. It doesn't matter if you got it to be ironic, nothing says old more than a nodding dog, a car air freshener shaped like a Christmas tree or a pair of furry dice.

#141 No Furry Seat Covers. They might keep your bum warm in the winter but they are like advertising that an old person owns the car. It's choosing comfort over style and that just isn't young so ditch the seat covers and drive faster to work up a sweat.

#142 No Matching Branded Clothing. Ok, so you've bought the Ferrari but there's no need to get the jacket and cap to match. You might as well stamp 'old' across your forehead instead.

#143 No Talking to Your Car in a Baby Voice. You might just be able to get away with referring to your car as a he or a she but you can never get away with stroking it or talking to it in a baby voice. It screams old and desperate.

144 Don't Go Thinking that Gut Is Normal

• • • • • • • • • • • • • • • •

Do you remember the first time you saw a naked old person? There you were, all young and smooth skinned and tight bodied, thinking that was normal because you looked like everybody on TV. And then there was the shock of how different the old person looked: big gut, droopy boobs, wobbly bum, *ewwww*.

Except now that you're the wobbly, droopy old person, it's all too easy to start thinking you look normal. Everybody's stomach sticks out like that! All thighs come packed with cellulite, everyone has a FUPA.

(FUPA, FYI, stands for Fat Upper Pubic Area, though some define it as the Fat Upper Pussy Area or Fat Upper Penile Area. It's . . . well, you know what it is.)

Except they don't. I'm not saying your body has to look like a twenty-eight-year-old's; I'm just asking that you be realistic about the changes time has wrought. And please, at the beach this summer, don't subject me to that gut flopping over a Speedo.

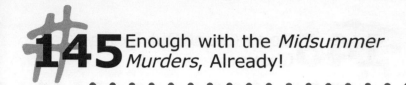

Maybe you faithfully sat in front of the TV every Thursday night (remember those pre-Sky+ days?) for the *Midsummer Murders* first series. Maybe you still catch the repeats nearly every night, the same way that your parents watch *The Six O'Clock News* and your kids watch *The Simpsons*. Maybe you've got the boxed sets as gifts over the past few years.

But listen, there can't be many people still alive in Midsummer, and John Nettles will soon be moving on. His departure from the show has already been announced – you've only got one more year . . .

12 OTHER CULTURAL REFERENCES SURE TO DATE YOU

M.A.S.H.

Profumo affair

Steptoe and Son

Are You Being Served?

Last of the Summer Wine

Charles and Diana's wedding

Porridge

The Falklands war

The Darling Buds of May

Happy Days

Dad's Army

Stop the bomb

146 Don't Count Out Exact Change

You've been there: in the queue behind the middle-aged woman who says, 'Wait a minute! I think I have the exact change!' and then proceeds to rummage through the recesses of her bag in search of the precise assortment of pennies that make up the price of her pop socks or chicken pot pie.

The reasoning seems to be that, if you pay for something with exact change, you at one stroke declutter your purse and get whatever you're buying for less. You've traded in all those heavy, jangly spare coins for a nourishing meat pie – and acted as if you're doing the poor cashier a big fat favour in the process.

But listen, change is inevitable. No matter how many pennies you get rid of, more will always come your way. And you're just annoying everybody in the meantime.

9 WAYS TO ANNOY OLD

1. Calculate the exact 10 per cent tip (you haven't heard or don't care that it's 15 per cent now).
2. Calculate the exact split of the bill.
3. Talk about the weather to strangers.
4. Ask the waiter or the shop assistant which entrée or pair of shoes you should get.
5. Call at 8:30 on Sunday morning, and act surprised that the other person is still asleep.
6. Send back your meal.
7. Be unable to find your wallet in your big old handbag or bulging jacket.
8. Excitedly get everybody to listen to you, and then forget what you were going to say.
9. Sit in your car for ever before pulling out of a parking space.

#147–160 How Not to Act Old at a Wedding

● ● ● ● ● ● ● ● ● ● ● ● ● ● ● ● ●

When you're young, you go to lots of weddings as all your friends get married. And then there's usually a dry spell for a couple of decades until your friends start getting *re*married and your friends' and siblings' and cousins' kids get hitched. Entering the second round of weddings, you may find you're a little out of practice. Plus, some of the rules of decorum and seemliness may have changed along with your age and status. Here, how not to be one of those mortifying old people.

#147 Don't Buy a New Outfit. You're not the bride. You're not a bridesmaid. You're not, God forbid, the mother (or father) of the bride, and you shouldn't dress like one. Just wear that nice outfit you wore to the last wedding you went to, even if it was eight years ago.

#148 Don't Wear Black. Somewhere in the eighties, when black reigned supreme, it was declared that it was now okay to wear black to weddings. But today, wearing black to a wedding, especially if you're of a certain age, just seems a trifle world-weary, which never sits well when you actually are. Conversely, though, do not wear a Nile green floral skirt suit that may cause the wedding party to suffer epileptic seizures.

#149 Don't Start Sobbing Midway through the ceremony whether from sentimental joy or true sorrow for anyone foolish enough to get married. Pull up your socks and keep it yourself.

#150 When They Ask Whether Anyone Has Just Cause to Stop the Wedding, keep quiet. See above.

#151 Do Not Attempt to Have Sex with a Bridesmaid or Usher. Leave those kinds of antics to the young people.

#152 Do Not Get Sloppy Drunk. Yes, I'm speaking to you, dear.

#153 Don't Take the Cake Too Seriously. Only old people go to weddings for the food.

#154 Don't Get Too Enthusiastic about the Macarena. At every wedding, there's always one middle-aged woman who it's all too clear doesn't get out to dance nearly enough. Every rendition of the Macarena, of 'Saturday Night Fever', of 'Let's Boogie Tonight' has her on her feet and in the middle of the floor, partner or not, even if everybody else is in the other room watching the cake get cut. Usually, that woman is me. But I swear I'm going to stop.

#155 Stop that Glass-clinking Stuff. It might be argued that bullying the bride and groom into kissing is not only lecherous but politically incorrect.

#156 Don't Skimp on Your Gift. Calculate the value of your gift based on the per-head cost of the wedding, which would probably be at least £50 these days.

#157 **But You Don't Have to Go Crazy.** Some modern weddings are so over-the-top – destination events that include several days of festivities – that buying a gift truly commensurate with the cost of your being there would be outrageous, especially when you consider the cost of getting to and being at the wedding. Be generous, but not as if you're trying to stay in the good graces of Don Corleone.

#158 **No Mama Drama.** Your niece's wedding is not the time to confront your sister-in-law about not bringing the right kind of pudding for Christmas dinner.

#159 **Don't Grab the Bouquet.** Let somebody truly optimistic catch it.

#160 **As Tracey Ullman Says, Go Home.** Leave the young people to dance the last dance and shut down the bar. Isn't it your bedtime?

161 Don't Watch the Evening News

When they claim that nobody watches the evening news on television anymore, I know for sure that's not true, because my parents-in-law watch it religiously every night. They're in their eighties. And have trouble getting out of the chair. But the evening news is a big deal for them.

I don't know a single person of my generation who watches it, though. We're too busy to sit down at 6 or 7, and we need our news for work, early in the morning or as it happens throughout the day. We do tend to read newspapers and magazines, though we may also check out the headlines online.

The Evil Young, of course, have declared a pogrom against both newspapers and commercial television. They get their news via RSS Feed, Twitter, or, if they're feeling extra-industrious, You-Tube. But watch the evening news? What for, since nothing on it is actually new?

162 Stop All that Moving Around

• • • • • • • • • • • • • • • • • •

Here's a counter-intuitive directive: if you want not to act old, you've got to knock off all that surfing, skating, basketball playing and cardio-kickboxing you've evidently been doing. Lying on the couch, staying out of the gym and sitting on the sidelines are the sports of the young, while middle-aged and older people are the ones who are joining ice-hockey teams and wearing themselves out on elliptical trainers.

So says a new study, which found that more and more middle-aged and older people are exercising and playing sports, while fewer young people are exercising now than were ten years ago. My scientific analysis: we've been doing all that kayaking and cycling in a misguided attempt to be thinner and more limber – aka younger – and to stave off dying. The evil young, meanwhile, say 'Ha! We're thin and limber without even trying. And we know we're never gonna die.'

Well, 'Ha!' back atcha, evil young. I now know there's an infinitely easier and more effective way to act younger: sit on my big fat arse. So long, spinning. Bye-bye, Bikram yoga. If I lounge here long enough, everybody's going to think I'm twenty-eight again.

163 Hold the Moo Goo Gai Pan

When we first tasted 'ethnic' food, what counted as exotic and exciting was some stew made of indefinable ingredients and bearing a funny name: moo goo gai pan, spaghetti puttanesca, pad Thai, the pu pu platter.

But in this era of McDonald's sushi (trust me; it's coming) and Indian frozen dinners, it's time to update your palate. Try the cold jelly Chengdu style. The kaiseki ryori. As long as you move beyond ordering the same thing you've been getting since you were nineteen, you'll be fine.

OLD FOOD/YOUNG FOOD: 18 CULINARY COMPARISONS

OLD FOOD	*YOUNG FOOD*
Prawn cocktail	Kumamoto oysters
Filet mignon	Hangar steak
Pork chop	Pork belly
Sauerbrauten	Kavalierspitz
Tuna tartare	Tuna cheek sashimi
Grilled swordfish	Arctic char, poached *sous vide*
Brunswick stew	Texas-style BBQ
Chicken teriyaki	Chicken lollipops
Spaghetti with clam sauce	Sea-urchin risotto
Aubergine parmigiana	Roasted ramps
Chardonnay	Muscadet
Fried eggs	Deep-fried poached egg
Tuna melt	Banh mi
White bread	Pain levain
Flan	Kulfi
Eclairs	Mochi
Ice cream	Pinkberry
Irish coffee	Dark & Stormy

164 Shave the Soul Patch

The age- and style-related migrations of men's facial hair remind me of the ups and downs of cars, say, or baby names. First, young men adopt some facial hair configuration – moustaches, for example, or mutton-chop sideburns – that old men think is outrageous. But then, over time, the fashion migrates up the age ladder, until the only guys wearing moustaches are middle-aged cops. Eventually, after even the middle-aged cops decide that 'staches are uncool and shave them off, the evil young start growing them again.

Beards, goatees, and various lengths and shapes of sideburns have made this journey over the past several decades, and right now the soul patch, long the epitome of youthful edginess, has become the look of fortyish web designers and hairdressers. Time to give the young back their hair patch.

12 THINGS YOU CAN'T EVEN THINK ABOUT WEARING (FOR MEN)

1. Tighty-whities.
2. Undershirts under your shirts.
3. A turtleneck of any kind.
4. A suit, unless you're going to a job interview or a funeral.
5. A camel-hair blazer.
6. Plaid anything, unless it's the shirt you bought in honour of Kurt Cobain.
7. Man jewellery. (Sorry, I have to take a hard line on this, but that's more my personal taste than any age-related prohibition. If your wife disagrees with me, you're allowed.)
8. A Spandex swimsuit. Really: too much information.
9. Both halves of the pyjamas.
10. Dad jeans. Just like Mum jeans: if they button around your waist, come from BHS, and have a relaxed fit, we don't care how cool you think you look – they're Dad jeans.
11. Tank tops.
12. Square-toed brown shoes with rubber soles and decorative stitching just like the ones your dad wears.

165 Stop Hoping Lauren Conrad Will Just Go Away

If you're wondering who Lauren Conrad is, you're worse off than I thought. Or better off: it might be preferable to live in blissful ignorance of Lauren, Heidi, Audrina, Spencer, Whitney and Brody (huh? who?) than to suffer the weekly – nay, daily, hourly – torture of wondering why Lauren *et al.* are famous and when they're just going to go away.

Never, that's when. And yes, Lauren and her friends are richer than you, they're treated more nicely, they get way more free goodies and fabulous job offers and they most certainly get lots more sex and love, too. Of course it's not fair, naturally you deserve it more, but hoping that the world will see the error of its ways and turn its attention from them to you is just, well, immature.

My recommendation: start watching *The Hills* (that's the show whose dramatic arc follows the real breaking of Lauren's real-life nail) and its New York counterpart, *The City*. While you're at it, catch up on your *Gossip Girl*. It may not be good for your soul, but it is good entertainment.

12 OTHER PEOPLE AND THINGS THAT WON'T DISAPPEAR ANYTIME SOON (NO MATTER HOW MUCH YOU WISH THEY WOULD)

1. Jeans as tight as leggings
2. Leggings instead of pants
3. Nose studs
4. Miniskirts
5. Hip-hop music
6. Reality TV
7. High-heeled ankle boots
8. Tops that make you look pregnant
9. *Family Guy*
10. Bikinis
11. iPods
12. Emoticons :(

166 Don't Be a Chicken

Old people certainly don't have a monopoly on fear. Some fears – spiders, public speaking, even flying – may even be ones we've faced and conquered. But change and novelty, not so much. The fear of newness even has a name: caicophobia.

Maybe you're afraid to try a different hair cut, since your current style has worked so well for you since 1993. Go on holiday in Virginia instead of Vermont? Undergo hypnosis, or attempt bungee jumping? Chicken, chicken, chicken, chicken. Not to mention the scariness inherent in doing something like moving across the country or changing careers, which forces you back into the position of being a rank beginner and therefore relatively ignorant and powerless, not a comfortable position for those of us who've achieved some measure of security and stature in our lives.

But being afraid to embrace the unknown can shorten your lifespan, at least if you're a rat. One study shows that scaredy-cat rats die sooner than adventuresome ones. You're safer bungee jumping than you are stressing over what will happen if you take the leap.

8 FEAR-CONQUERING IDEAS

IF YOU'RE AFRAID OF . . .	*TRY . . .*
Going back to school	Teaching a class
Moving to a city apartment	Renting an apartment for a holiday
Going into the weight room	Hiring a trainer
Building a website	Starting a blog
Setting up Sky+	Joining PC World Online
Going on holiday alone	Going on a singles tour
Wearing a bathing suit at the beach	Swimming for exercise
Having anal sex	Wearing a chastity belt

167 Step Away from the Giant Pumpkin

• • • • • • • • • • • • • • • • • • •

One of the fascinating and bizarre things I've noticed recently is that middle-aged men love to grow giant pumpkins. Not a few guys in some isolated pumpkin patch, mind you, but a whole 'giant pumpkin community' that spans the globe, organizes scores of competitions every autumn and even hosts an annual convention.

Is it coincidence that most giant pumpkin enthusiasts are men in their fifties? I think not. People in their fifties seem to take up all sorts of weird hobbies and enthusiasms, from cultivating hydrangeas to investigating the family tree to collecting painted tin dachshunds to developing a gourmet cuisine based entirely on seaweed.

I guess this is what happens when the kids are grown, the mortgage is paid off and you've decided not to get a dog or a divorce. Everything else has been scratched off your life list, and what's left? 'Instead of having an affair, leaving you, or getting hair plugs, I'm just going to grow a pumpkin as big as a fucking house, honey. Don't wait up.'

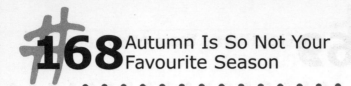

168 Autumn Is So Not Your Favourite Season

Favourite season of the old: autumn. Why? Because the colours are so lovely, you get to wear clothes that cover your body again, and you're forced to stay in the house and eat beef stew and apple pie and drink sidecars.

Sounds pretty good to me, but not to the young. For young people, fall means a return to school (blech) even years after they've graduated. No more bikinis, no more sex on the beach, goodbye to the summer share. Second and third place go to spring, as in fever, and winter, for the snowboarding and the nice Christmas cheque from Mum and Dad.

So that leaves the old with autumn all to themselves.

8 OTHER FAVOURITES YOU MAY WANT TO RETHINK

1. **Favourite Colour:** Greyish-green.
2. **Favourite Holiday:** Mother's Day.
3. **Favourite Day of the Week:** Thursday. Or maybe Sunday.
4. **Favourite Music:** Classical. Or maybe jazz.
5. **Favourite Vegetable:** Brussels sprouts.
6. **Favourite City:** Winchester.
7. **Favourite Skirt Style:** Pleated.
8. **Favourite Weather:** Cool and rainy.

169 Get Rid of the Harley

Having just returned from a 700-mile road trip, I can tell you with certainty that every motorcyclist on the American highway is at least fifty-six years old. All the biker babes have Nice 'n Easy covering their grey and pot bellies straining against their leather pants. Motorcyclists may think that roaring along on a hog makes them look cool, or young, but as an elderly vehicle of choice, bikes are right up there with campervans.

How did motorcyles go from being a symbol of youthful rebellion to one of middle-aged desperation? The timeline begins with Marlon Brando looking young and hot in *The Wild One* in 1953. Hippies and bikers united in their countercultural beliefs in the 1960s – until Altamont. A fan was killed, a riot ensued, and the image of motorcyclists went from cool to terrifying in two seconds flat.

It got even weirder after that, when a band of Hells Angels plotted to kill Mick Jagger, attacking the Hamptons by boat.

These image problems discouraged young people from taking up motorcycling over the past few decades, so now most of the active motorcyclists are middle-aged or older. If it's youthfulness you're after, trade in that hog for something more daring, like racing junk. Or a fixed-gear bicycle: look Ma, no brakes!

14 THINGS THAT USED TO BE YOUNG BUT ARE NOW OLD

1. Leather jackets
2. Folk music
3. VW Beetles
4. Modern dance
5. Sausalito
6. Cigarettes
7. Group-therapy sessions
8. Hamburgers
9. Astrology
10. The Grateful Dead
11. Berets
12. Black turtlenecks
13. Wine
14. Sweets

17 THINGS THAT USED TO BE OLD BUT ARE NOW YOUNG

1. Hair dye
2. Bow ties
3. Bob Dylan
4. Manhattans
5. Politics
6. Hermès scarves
7. Fords
8. Pigs in blankets
9. Poetry
10. Las Vegas
11. Tea
12. Cigars
13. Big formal weddings
14. Big glasses
15. Poker
16. Hats
17. Rubber galoshes

170 No, that Was Not Mary-Kate Olsen You Saw on the Number 66 Bus

First off, it's Mary-Kate and *Ashley*. Secondly, you can too tell them apart. Mary-Kate is a little shorter, skinnier, darker haired and all over pointier. And if that still isn't clear, in breaking news, Spencer Pratt told *US Weekly* that Mary-Kate is 'the less cute twin'.

The Olsen twins, for those who spent the past few decades on the planet Xebo, jointly played the baby on a show called *Full House* and went on to become billionaires by doing something visible only to eleven-year-old girls. And while they certainly seem to be everywhere, everywhere does not include your suburban commuter bus. Nor did you see one or both of them in your local pizza shop (they subsist on air) or trying on shoes in Sports Direct.

The faux sighting of vaguely familiar baby celebrities is a common failing of the old. Yes, they all look alike. But that young, sweet, too thin girl you saw on your local commuter bus was just the waif next door.

171 Don't Have Black Friends, Gay Friends, Guy Friends, Jewish Friends, or Young Friends

• • • • • • • • • • • • • • • • • •

Or white friends, straight friends, girl friends, Baptist friends, or old friends.

No, I am not a racist, homophobic, sexist, anti-Semitic, ageist freak. What I'm saying is that *calling* your friends 'my black friends' or 'my gay friends' is evidence that you're conscious of your friends as belonging to some special group, which is an outmoded way of looking at things. Friends are friends, and the modern – dare I say young – way is to accept people as individuals and not identify them as anything other than 'my friends'.

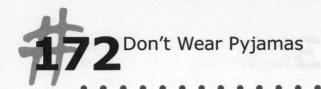
172 Don't Wear Pyjamas

One day soon, pyjamas are going to take their place in the fashion archives alongside girdles, sock garters, and ascot ties. Pyjamas are the nightwear of the aging – male as well as female. While teenage girls may go through a short-lived cute-nightwear phase, for the most part pyjamas are being replaced by sweatpants, underwear, or just plain skin.

So turn those pyjama trousers into office wear. Pair the tops with jeans and blazers. And at bedtime, lock the kids out and show up naked. If your spouse complains, say I made you do it.

173 Gotta Love those *Entourage* Boys

● ● ● ● ● ● ● ● ● ● ● ● ● ● ●

I was walking down the street the other day – yes, right here in New Jersey – and there coming towards me were Vince, Turtle, Drama, Ari and E. I tried waving to them, then leaping in front of them and finally, in a desperate bid for their attention, whipped off my turtleneck, tracksuit trousers, and underwear and stood in their path wearing only my Garnet Hill polka-dotted knee-socks and Blundstone ankle boots. Finally, they glanced my way.

'She's yours, Turtle,' said Vince.

'No, no,' I said. 'I just want to ask you a question.'

'Questions start at $20 million,' snapped Ari.

'C'mon, Ari,' said Vince, rousing himself to blink. 'She's just a fan.'

'Oh, Jeez,' said Drama, 'she can't be a fan. If she's really a fan, we're over, over! Look at her, she's older than Tina Fey!'

'Oh, yeah?' said Turtle. 'I bet she's not too old to suck my cock. How about it, Granny?'

'Please, I wouldn't suck your little finger if it had chocolate frosting all over it and I'd been on a sugar fast for a month,' I said, hoping he wouldn't guess it took me a whole twenty-four hours to come up with that line. 'And I'm not a fan; I watch you only in a desperate attempt to bond with my husband and teenage son. But what I want to know is why they love you so much.'

'They love us because they wish they were us,' said E. 'We're proof that everything you've ever told them is wrong is actually right; you can be your most immature, lazy, stupid, unredeemed self, and you'll get rich and famous for it. Oh, and you'll get lots and lots of great sex with babes who are young and gorgeous and never make you put your Coke can in the recycling.'

'So do you horrify and repulse me because I'm female? Or because I'm old and out of it?'

'That's two questions,' said Ari, yelling at me through his mobile phone, even though we weren't actually on the phone. '$40 million!'

The other guys looked at each other and shrugged. 'All the other women love us,' they said. 'Must be the old thing.'

'But I would have hated you even when I was young,' I said.

Too late, though: a Ferrari pulled up carrying some rappers, some pole dancers and a couple of pit bulls, and the guys were off. But before they pulled away, Vince looked back at me over his shoulder and called, 'See you next Sunday night?'

I sighed. 'Sure.'

174 No Bras the Size of Scotland

As the years advance, we full-figured gals have a, ahem, weighty challenge ahead of us. How do we hoist the girls as high as possible without resorting to a bra the size of Scotland?

The answer, as with so many things, is money. Any bra that's going to do its considerable job and still look feminine, attractive and young is going to set you back at least as much as you just spent on trainers for your teenager. You're going to have to go to a fancy lingerie department to buy it, and even be fitted by a trained professional brandishing a tape measure.

Let's just quickly run over the elements your bra *cannot* have: elastic thick and strong enough to support a bungee jumper; more than two – or, in extreme cases, three – hooks in back; cups so capacious they totally rule out the possibility of cleavage; no quadriboob; no backfat.

At the same time, your bra needs to lift, separate, streamline, steady and smooth. Impossible? No. Expensive but worth it? Absolutely.

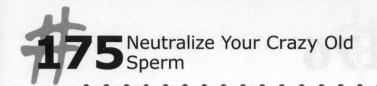

#175 Neutralize Your Crazy Old Sperm

A new study that shows that children of fathers over fifty-five are more likely to develop bipolar disorder and other mental illnesses. Maternal age, I hasten to point out to all you guys out there who try to blame women for everything, was not a factor.

Finally, a solid reason – beyond, you know, imminent decay and death – for older guys to put some limits on how long they go around spraying out babies. Why anyone would want to make it through the enormous job of raising a family only to go out and raise another one is totally beyond me, unless you're the kind of guy who wasn't much involved in raising the first batch of kids and won't do much about raising the second or third batches, either.

Of course, you might believe that your sperm, mutant as it is, still deserves to flourish wherever it finds purchase. If so, I'm going to hunt you down and neutralize you myself.

#176 Don't Fear the Birthday

• • • • • • • • • • •

Of course it sucks to see those numbers mount up. But don't deny the birthday. Look at it this way: nobody has to know how old you are to justify a celebration. By this point in life we all know we have to seize pleasure and attention whenever and however we can get it – which is never often enough.

So don't shy away from the dinner, the party, the presents, the cake and, yes, even a big blazing forest of candles to mark another successful year of holding your head up high.

MADLIBS: HOW TO CELEBRATE YOUR BIRTHDAY RIGHT

To have a really great birthday party, invite _____ of your closest
                                                      number

friends to_____. Serve _____ and_____, and
           place   kind of drink   kind of food

decorate the place with lots of _____ and _____. A theme,
                                 plural noun   plural noun

such as _____ or _____, can help make the event more _____.
         animals   colour   adjective

Be sure to play _____ and sing _____. Everyone has
                 game   name of song

to _____the birthday boy or girl. Don't forget to open the gifts;
   verb

people will enjoy watching your reaction to such items as _____
                                                           plural

_____ and _____. And for the final touch, try to blow
noun   plural noun

out all _____ _____ on your _____ cake.
         number   plural noun   adjective

177 Stifle the Rants

• • • • • • • • • • • • • • • • • • •

Men of all ages like their rants and their moans, and that tendency only increases as the years go by. Get a middle-aged guy in front of an audience, be it a lecture hall or his poor captive wife, and chances are he will rant: about the stupidity of politicians and corporations, about the inequities of the monetary system, about his children and his neighbours, about the world at large and the heavens above.

According to unscientific studies conducted in my own living room, older men do this as a way to show off the superior power of their vocal chords relative to their waning upper-body strength. They do it to sound smart and smug and to throw their weight around without risking any actual bloodshed.

But I'm here to tell you, guys (and rant-inclined girls): can the rants if you don't want to act old. Do not, no matter how inspired you feel, carry on about any of the following:

- The ridiculousness of contemporary baby names, epitomized by the child – you swear: your sister-in-law the nurse saw it with her own eyes – who was named Gonorrhea.
- The failure of young people today to move out of their parents' houses, get married, and assume adult responsibilities before the age of, say, 43.
- The inflated cost of jeans. Why, you bought the very jeans you're wearing at Gap eleven years ago, and they still look perfectly *fine*, except for that tiny coffee stain near the crotch!

What are you supposed to do instead? Assume the lotus position, focus your third eye, and if someone asks what you think of the new tax scheme or the latest reality show, chant, 'It's all good.'

178 Don't Go Hatin' on Christmas

Hating Christmas is an affliction peculiar to the old. Why? Let me count the ways.

- It's expensive, and we have to pay for it.
- It's a lot of work, and we have to do all of it.
- We are really, really, *really* sure there's no Santa.
- There was that time we got drunk and had a huge fight with our spouse on Christmas Eve. Also, that other time. And the time when our mother-in-law started screaming at us about not getting her a nice enough present. And the time we threw up in the mashed potatoes. And the time . . . oh, never mind. The point is once you've been around for enough Christmases, you accumulate plenty of bad memories along with the good.
- It's cold, and we no longer like the cold.
- It's almost never a white Christmas, and if it is, we have to shovel it.
- We're exhausted.
- We have too much work to do as it is.
- Nobody ever wants to kiss us under the mistletoe.

We could go on, but we're getting kind of fed up already. Let's just say we have our reasons for hating Christmas, and they're good ones, but at the same time we're making ourselves seem, not to mention feel, older by being such Scrooges.

How to renovate your Xmas outlook?

Well, you could slip a diamond into your own Christmas stocking. Surprise everyone on Christmas Eve with tickets to Barbados and nothing for Christmas dinner in the refrigerator. Give all your money to a worthy charity and so create inner peace and an iron-clad excuse for skipping the whole damn thing in one stroke of genius.

Or just develop an appreciation for single-malt scotch and chocolate-chip meringues, and pass the season in an alcohol-and-sugar haze. Here's the recipe:

Chocolate-chip Meringue Cookies

Ingredients

2 large egg whites

$^1/_8$ teaspoon cream of tartar

110g granulated sugar

1 tablespoon cocoa powder (optional)

1 teaspoon vanilla extract

250g dark chocolate chips or chocolate chunks (or even M&Ms)

Directions

Preheat oven to 140°C. Line 2 cookie sheets with parchment paper.

With electric mixer on high, beat egg whites until foamy. Add cream of tartar and beat until soft peaks form. Add sugar slowly, beating until stiff but not dry peaks form. (The whole 'stiff peaks' thing sometimes fails me here, but never mind. Beat till it seems like they're as stiff as they're ever going to be, then give up and carry on.)

Beat in cocoa powder and vanilla. Fold in chocolate chips. Bake until completely firm and dry, but still white, about 35–45 minutes; you should be able to lift cookies from the paper. You can turn off the oven but leave meringues inside for an hour if you like crunchier meringues.

179 Don't Post Yourself on Youporn

Okay, if you've never had a look at youporn.com, all I'm going to say is DON'T GO TO THE SITE IF YOU'RE AT WORK OR ANYONE ELSE IS ANYWHERE NEAR YOU, ALL RIGHT? This is a strict warning. DO NOT, under any circumstances, disobey me.

Jeez, you disobeyed, didn't you? As you undoubtedly saw, the second you clicked on youporn's home page, it's hardcore and free from the opening act on. Billed as the YouTube of pornography, with user-contributed 'home' videos, everything I've watched on the site – strictly for research purposes, mind you – has looked suspiciously professional.

Or maybe it's just hard for me to believe that women *that* young, pretty, big-breasted, flat-stomached, and with such tidy lightning bolts shaved into their pubic hair are actually amateurs.

I'm going to assume, however, that you are a real person who does not work in the sex trade. And I'm going to tell you that, no matter how inspired you may feel to post your own antics on youporn, desist. No one wants to see your paunch, your thatch, or the results of your Viagra binge on any screen, large or small.

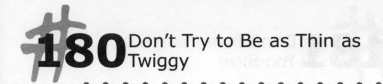

180 Don't Try to Be as Thin as Twiggy

At thirteen, I aspired to have a figure like Twiggy's – and I wasn't far off, either. Twiggy and I were both built like, well, twigs, and keeping that thin was disgustingly effortless.

Well, things have changed, and even Twiggy isn't immune from middle-aged spread; she limits her diet to one chocolate square at a time, she says, and 'one pudding a month' or risks bloating up like every other over-forty.

There goes the myth of the naturally thin person who stays that way for ever. If even Twiggy porks up, what hope is there for the rest of us?

Extra non-diet tip: don't reference Twiggy in relation to thinness, weight loss, or modelling. Young people won't have any idea who you're talking about. Kate Moss, maybe. Doutzen or Agyness (born Laura) Deyn: now you're talking.

181 Don't Drive Too Fast . . . or Too Slow

● ● ● ● ● ● ● ● ● ● ● ● ● ● ●

The cartoon old person crawls down the road in their outsized car, hunched over the wheel, riding the brake, a long line of cars trailing in frustration behind.

But in reality the old driver is nearly as likely to drive too fast as too slow. Freed from earth's surly bonds, unhobbled by arthritic knees or shortness of breath, the aged often step on the accelerator and ignore speed limits and traffic regulations.

Of course, you fit neither of these antiquated stereotypes, do you? Of course not. You always see every sign, you never get lost, and you absolutely noticed that car you backed into last week – you just didn't feel like stopping, that's all. Which reminds me of a joke:

One day Harvey and Moe, two old and aged friends, went out for a drive. They came to a stop sign and Harvey sailed right through. Moe was nervous but didn't say anything. They came to another stop sign, and again, Harvey didn't even slow down. Then they came to a red light, and Harvey just kept going, barely avoiding oncoming cars.

Finally Moe had to say something. 'Harvey,' he said, 'why didn't you stop at those stop signs and that red light?'

'Oh,' Harvey said. 'Am I driving?'

#182 Don't Talk to Strangers

Maybe what happened is that everybody up to the age of, oh, thirty had the 'Don't talk to strangers' directive drilled so hard into their heads that it's second nature for them to keep to themselves. In airports, in kickboxing class, in the queue at the bank, they tend to keep their eyes trained on their phones or the mirror and not to make eye contact or strike up animated casual conversations.

Not the way that we do – or at least that I do. I'll talk to anybody, anywhere. In fact, I'm often looking for the chance to swap comments on train schedules or coffee orders or whether that skirt we're both trying on is flattering. Finding myself alone on an aeroplane or in a restaurant, I'm likely to walk out with a new friend.

However, that new friend is unlikely to be under forty. And if I start talking to strangers in the vicinity of my children, they react as if I spontaneously started dancing and singing 'Let's Get It On' right there in the street.

So if you want not to act old, stop making those random comments in yoga class or asking the woman in the waiting room whether she likes the book she's reading. But if you want to stay happy, just keep doing it when no one young is watching.

183 No Arcade Fire or Porkpie Hats

It's one thing for an ancient (that's you, baby) to keep abreast (there's an old word) of popular culture and stay aware of what the young and hipsterish are doing just to torture you.

But it's quite another to attempt to actually be a hipster. You may think you can deconstruct all the elements of hipsterhood – the Yoo-hoo T-shirts and the Regina Spektor tapes (yeah, they're back), the vegan diet and the loft in Williamsburg and the toddler named Leta – and then you will be a hipster. But you're forgetting the most important thing it takes to be a hipster; you have to be young.

How young? If you have to ask: younger than you. So give it up, dollface. Put the aviator shades in the case, find a long-sleeved shirt to cover up the crown o' thorns inked on your bicep and stop calling everything fierce.

You're sure to win as much admiration for all your acquired wisdom as you did for your mint green Vespa, right? As *if*.

8 ITEMS OF HIPSTER GEAR YOU CAN GET AWAY WITH

1. Granddad cardigan
2. Orthopaedic sandals from Germany
3. Skinny tie
4. Ray-Ban sunglasses with prescription lenses
5. Heavy beard
6. Ranch house in Portland, Oregon
7. Stocking cap
8. Dress worn over jeans

8 ITEMS OF HIPSTER GEAR YOU CAN'T

1. Cosby sweater
2. Motorcycle boots from Germany
3. Keffiyeh scarf
4. Ray-Ban frames with clear lenses
5. Mussed-up hair
6. Loft in Bed-Stuy
7. Flip-rim hat
8. Shorts worn over stockings

184 Don't Walk Small

Here's, ahem, one step to looking and feeling younger instantly; take big steps. That's right – biiiiiiig, wide, bold steps. Go ahead, try it. It really is like magic.

And once you start walking bigger, you'll be amazed to realize that you've been shuffling around with those little timid I-have-to-be-careful-or-I-could topple over-and-break-a-hip steps. You'll see that, with most people, steps get smaller and smaller with each passing year, with teenagers walking like the Keep on Truckin' guy and your grandma mincing along like a ballerina *en pointe*.

Keep on truckin', baby.

185 Don't Die. Or Even Consider the Possibility of Dying

During the three or four hours I spent last night in casualty (don't ask; you know I am forbidden by the Rules of Not Acting Old to talk about my health), I read a really great passage in a novel called *In The Woods* by Tana French that goes like this:

'We think about death so little, these days, except to flail hysterically at it with trendy forms of exercise and high-fiber cereals and nicotine patches . . . Now death is uncool, old-fashioned.'

Death is uncool; I love it! It's absolutely true. Death is so not done these days that, unless your brain stem has been removed and you're older than, say, 105, you can never ever admit that dying might lie somewhere in your future.

Death is more uncool than flabby jowls, more uncool than cellulite, more uncool even than wearing your trousers belted just under your manboobs. Death is more uncool than driving a Lincoln, more uncool than talking about your gallbladder operation, more uncool than smoking cigars around the baby.

What's more, dying is a deliberately uncool act, like walking into John Lewis and buying yourself a pair of grey plastic crocs and wearing them with pop socks and culottes. I mean, how dare you be so clueless? Haven't you heard of Pilates? Super-low-calorie diets and red wine? Energy-field healing? Seat belts? Dying: there's no damn excuse!

If you want not to act old, you've got to behave as the young do – as if you're going to live for ever. But unlike the young, who can skip dinner and knock back six martinis and dance till five and then go to work at eight, you've got to drink nothing stronger than Vitamin Water and get at least seven hours sleep to feel as if you're not going to drop dead right on the spot. But even a life that's no longer worth living is better than death, the ultimate uncool.

7 COOL WAYS TO DIE (IF YOU MUST)

1. Crash your motorcycle off cliff
2. Get trampled by mob of crazed fans
3. Be eaten by shark while surfing world's most treacherous wave
4. Have heart attack while having sex with twenty-three-year-old twin bullfighters
5. Be thrown by wild steer in rodeo competition
6. Get shot in neck by poisoned dart while functioning as double agent
7. Throw self in front of bus to save innocent orphan

7 UNCOOL WAYS TO DIE

1. Have heart attack while having sex with a prostitute
2. Get hit by bus while rooting through bag to find your mobile phone
3. Smothered in your sleep by your overweight, blind cat
4. Have aneurysm while berating your spouse
5. Overdose on anti-cholesterol meds
6. Your life becomes so boring that your heart loses interest in beating
7. Start to cross street and forget to make it to the other side

Acknowledgements

An old person could never develop a website and write a book called *How Not to Act Old* without considerable help.

My first thanks go to my smart, funny, graphically astute and insightful research assistant Danielle Miksza, who was my main spy in the house of the young and aid in turning the blog into this book. Danielle told me what young people drank on Saturday night and how old people acted on Monday morning, among many other inside details that found their way into this text.

My children, Rory, Joe and Owen Satran, also provided essential help and research. When I first started the blog, Joe would come home from his summer job at the *Huffington Post* to tell me how to code my pictures so they'd float inside the text. A knowledgeable foodie, he helped parse the list of old food and young food in the book. Owen provided my very first blog entry – who over twenty ever heard, never mind said, the words 'Yo, you copped fire, son'? – and also detailed the difference between a brotha and a bro. And my daughter Rory, though she still won't be my friend on Facebook, did help me figure out how not to Facebook old and also came up with my hilarious subtitle.

I'm lucky enough to have an awesome – and I don't say that lightly – agent, Deborah Schneider, who not only loved the blog from the start but found me a fabulous book detail mere weeks after I launched. Thank you, Deborah.

If I were to design my ideal publisher – just one of my megalomaniacal fantasies – it would surely be HarperCollins, with its books that manage to combine beauty and brains and fun and edginess: hey, much like myself! Thank you in particular to my initial editor Nancy Miller, long-lost friend and colleague of my youth, and to Jennifer Schulkind, who brought fresh enthusiasm and ideas to the project. I'd also like to thank assistant editor Molly Lindley and publishers Mary Ellen O'Neill and Carrie Kania.

My friends, colleagues and readers of the blog helped me believe I should keep exploring the subject and contributed their own experiences for my amusement and the edification of all. Also, a couple hundred of my loved ones contributed wonderful title ideas, though I ended up doing, as usual, what I wanted to do from the beginning.

I'd like to especially thank the fabulous photographer Alexa Garbarino, who helped me figure out what this book might look like; Christina Baker Kline, who loved it from the beginning; Dorothea Benton Frank, who sent it to so many people it found its way to Meg Cabot; Meg Cabot, who blogged about it, sending thousands of her fans my way, and then blurbed it; Laurie Lico Albanese, always ready with good sense and inspiration; Alice Elliott Dark, who told me about walking large and FUPAs; Hugh Hunter, who told me that I and all my aged friends had to learn to dial and type with our thumbs; Diana Biederman, for the '21' Club splendour; Rita DiMatteo, who told me planning was old (undoubtedly while we were planning something together); Judy Coyne, for inspiring me to write like this in the first place and who, with the lovely Lesley Jane Seymour, adapted it for *More* magazine; and my husband Dick Satran, who kept reminding me to make it funny, not depressing.

Fellow bloggers and friends who helped spread the word include the inspirational Debbie Galant of Baristanet; Holly Cara Price of snoopdujour.com; Jen Singer, who writes for *Good Housekeeping*; Mauigirl52; and Rob Robinson of thinktrain.net, who called me 'Stuff Old People Like', which still tickles. Anya Streitman and Verena Von Pfetten of the *Huffington Post* gave me a platform outside my own venue. My writing partners Linda Rosenkrantz and Kimberly Bonnell always delight and illuminate and support, whether we're working together or not.

Obviously, a book that starts out as a blog includes a lot more ideas and opinions than your usual nearly solo effort. Others I'd like to acknowledge include Henry Seltzer, Deborah and Dana Jennings, Cathy Gleason, Sheila Weller, Elliot Pinsley and Leslie Brody, Dave and Christina Baker Kline, Alexis Romay, Eric Levin, Toni Martin, Amy Edelman and to the extraordinary photographer Fran Liscio for suggesting an LOL title that I hope someday will find its rightful book: *I Scored Some Eileen Fisher Caftans and That Shit Was Bangin'*.